D0671048

PRAYING THE MASS

A Guide to the New English Translation of the Mass

PRAYING THE MASS

The Prayers of the People

Jeffrey Pinyan

The diocese of Metuchen has determined that ecclesiastical approval is not required for this book.

First Edition, Copyright © 2009 Jeffrey Pinyan
Second Edition, Copyright © 2010 Jeffrey Pinyan
All rights reserved

Unless otherwise noted, the Scripture citations used in this work are taken from
the *Revised Standard Version Bible—Second Catholic Edition* (Ignatius Edition)
© 2006 National Council of the Churches of Christ in the USA.
Used with permission. All rights reserved.

Excerpts from the English translation of the *Catechism of the Catholic Church, Second Edition*
© 1994 and 1997, Libreria Editrice Vaticana and the United States Conference
of Catholic Bishops. Used with permission. All rights reserved.

Excerpts from *The Spirit of the Liturgy*
© 2000, Ignatius Press.
Used with permission. All rights reserved.

Excerpts from the Latin text of the *Ordo Missae I*
© 2008 from the *Missale Romanum* third typical edition.
All rights reserved.

Excerpts from the English translation of *The Order of Mass*
© 2008, International Committee on English in the Liturgy, Inc.
All rights reserved.

English translations of the documents of the Second Vatican Council, papal documents,
and other Vatican documents are from the Vatican website, http://www.vatican.va/.

TheCrossReference@gmail.com
www.PrayingTheMass.com

Contents

Acknowledgements . . . . *i*

Foreword . . . . *ii*

Introduction 1

1. Preparing for Prayer 15

      Personal Prayer   15

      Reading the Bible   18

      The Eucharistic Fast   20

      Sacramental Confession   21

      Silence and Stillness   22

2. Sign of the Cross 25

3. Common Responses and Postures 33

      "Amen."   33

      "And with your spirit."   34

      Standing   36

      Sitting   37

      Kneeling   37

      Bowing   39

      Genuflecting   40

4. Penitential Act 43

      Form A, "I confess…"   44

      Form B   47

      Form C   48

      "Lord, have mercy."   48

      Sprinkling with Holy Water   49

5. The *Gloria* 53

6. Liturgy of the Word 59

      "Thanks be to God."   59

      Responsorial Psalm or Gradual 61

      Gospel Acclamation   63

      "Glory to you, O Lord."   63

      "Praise to you, Lord Jesus Christ." 65

7. Profession of Faith 69

      Apostles' Creed   71

      Nicene Creed   74

8. Prayer of the Faithful 99

9. Offertory Prayers **105**

        Offertory Procession   106

        "Blessed be God forever."   107

        "May the Lord accept…"   108

10. Eucharistic Prayer **115**

        Preface Dialogue   116

        Holy, Holy, Holy   118

        Consecration   121

        The Mystery of Faith   123

        "Amen."   127

11. Communion Rite **131**

        Our Father   132

        "For the kingdom…"   136

        Sign of Peace   140

        Lamb of God   142

        "Lord, I am not worthy…"   144

        Holy Communion   147

12. Concluding Rite **153**

        Dialogue   154

        Final Blessing   155

        Dismissal   156

Appendix **159**

Bibliography 164

Acknowledgments

I am indebted to two priests whose blogs on the Church and her liturgy I read religiously. Thanks to Rev. John Zuhlsdorf at *What Does the Prayer Really Say?*, I have come to appreciate the importance of good translations and better explanations, and thanks to Rev. Tim Finigan at *The Hermeneutic of Continuity*, I have learned how necessary it is to look at the Church's liturgy through the eyes of her tradition. Through them, my eyes were opened to the beauty and heritage of the whole of Catholic tradition (both before and after Vatican II).

I thank my wife Kristin for putting up with me while I was writing this, my oldest brother Rev. Charlie for his loving and faithful service to the Church and his spiritual assistance to me, and my parents for raising me in a home where attending Mass was not a chore (even if it took me a while to realize it).

I thank the contributors to the *New Liturgical Movement*, especially Shawn Tribe, Rev. Thomas Kocik, and Deborah Morlani. I also thank Rev. Martin Miller from Princeton University for the homily he gave which provided me with the quote from C.S. Lewis to begin the chapter on the Creed. The hands on the cover are those of Raymond Ip, a friend from my parish. I am also grateful for those friends and acquaintances who proofread the book and critically reviewed it.

I owe a special debt of gratitude to Michael Dubruiel (1958-2008), whose *The How-to Book of the Mass* was a major inspiration for this work. May the Lord grant him to find mercy on that Day, giving his soul rest in the peace of Christ, forever singing praise to God and to the Lamb.

Last, but not least, I thank His Holiness Pope Benedict XVI, whose writings before and after his election to the papacy moved me to study and love all of the liturgies of the Catholic Church.

This book is dedicated to all the lay saints of the Church.

Foreword

It is with great pleasure and fraternal pride that I welcome you to this immensely useful and inspiring work. Great pleasure – because I am sure that those who read it will be edified in their approach to participating at Mass. Fraternal pride – because the author is my younger brother and godson!

In 1992, at my Mass of Thanksgiving the day following my ordination to the priesthood, altar server Jeffrey helped lead the way as the crucifer. Now it is my turn to lead the way into a great work of faith on his part.

Praying the Mass is a helpful and accessible volume for anyone who would like to enter more deeply into the experience of the Eucharistic liturgy. And it is especially useful because of the pending implementation of the new translation of the Roman Missal.

Jeffrey skillfully weaves together theology, history and spirituality to explain why we pray, how we pray and what we pray at Mass. While this book is written primarily to guide lay people, I expect that priests and deacons will also find much to nourish their own prayerful participation at Mass as well.

In his 2009 homily on the Solemnity of Corpus Christi, Pope Benedict warned of the risk of "a formal and empty Eucharistic worship, in celebrations lacking this participation from the heart that is expressed in veneration and respect for the liturgy." This book contributes to the movement to stir "participation from the heart" and is most timely indeed.

Rev. Charles Pinyan
Solemnity of the Most Holy Body and Blood of Christ, 2009

INTRODUCTION
What is "praying the Mass"?

THE MASS, OR AS it is called in the Eastern Rites, the "Divine Liturgy,"[1] is the greatest prayer that can be prayed, because it is the prayer of Jesus Christ to God the Father. Christ is the Head of His Church – His Mystical Body, the People of God – so the faithful who participate in the Mass are also praying that same prayer, each to his own degree. Because the priest by virtue of his participation in the **ordained** (ministerial) priesthood acts *in persona Christi* ("in the person of Christ"), there are certain parts of the Mass which are prayed by him alone; but because all the faithful share in the **baptismal** (common) priesthood, we are called to participate in the Mass in our own way.

During the Mass, the saints and angels in Heaven are present in a mystical way, because the Mass is a foretaste of the true heavenly liturgy. Participation in the Mass is not hindered by death: the souls of the faithful departed also being purified benefit from the offering of Mass. The Mass is truly the action of the whole Church joined with Christ.

Every Mass is offered for four reasons (or "ends"): first, to give glory to God; second, to thank Him for all He has bestowed; third, to

---

[1] The word "liturgy" comes from the Greek *leitourgos*, meaning "public work" or "work on behalf of the people." In calling worship the *Divine* Liturgy, the Eastern tradition emphasizes the origin and direction of worship while affirming our necessary (human) participation in it.

attain expiation for our sins by means of repentance and the offering of the Most Holy Sacrifice of the Body and Blood of Jesus Christ (the Eucharist) to the Father; and fourth, to present our needs before God in prayers of petition. In order for the Mass to be what it is meant to be, it is necessary that the faithful cooperate with and take part in the Mass through *individual participation* in it.

Actual Participation

The Second Vatican Council, following in the footsteps of Pope St. Pius X, Pope Pius XI, and Pope Pius XII, impressed upon the Church the need for a renewed commitment to participation in the Church's liturgy. This was made clear in 1963 in the *first* document promulgated by the Council, the Constitution on the Sacred Liturgy (CSL), which praised the liturgy as "the summit towards which the activity of the Church is directed" as well as "the font from which all her power flows." (CSL 10) Because participation in the liturgy is "the primary and indispensable source from which the faithful are to derive the true Christian spirit" (CSL 14) each Catholic must strive to participate in the liturgy to the best of his or her ability. Vatican II characterized this participation as *"plenam, consciam, atque actuosam"* (CSL 14), that is, "full, conscious, and actual" (or "… active").[2]

This language can be found in an instruction on sacred music in the liturgy from Pope St. Pius X in 1903, *Tra la sollecitudini* (TLS). Pope Pius wrote that the faithful acquire "the true Christian spirit … from its foremost and indispensible font, which is the active participation in the [liturgy]." At the time, he was concerned primarily with the restoration of Gregorian chant "so that the faithful may again take a more active part" (TLS 3) in the Church's liturgy.

Pope Pius XI echoed the sentiments of his predecessor regarding the congregation participating in the Mass with Gregorian chant twenty-five years later in an Apostolic Constitution:

> In order that the faithful may more *actively participate in divine worship*, let them be made once more to sing the Gregorian Chant,

---

[2] The translation of *actuosa* as "active" can lead to a misunderstanding of the word. Pope Benedict XVI, in his post-synodal Apostolic Exhortation *Sacramentum Caritatis*, linked *actuosa* to *authentica*, that is, "actual" and "authentic" participation.

so far as it belongs to them to take part in it. It is most important that when the faithful assist at the sacred ceremonies, or when pious sodalities take part with the clergy in a procession, *they should not be merely detached and silent spectators*, but, filled with a deep sense of the beauty of the Liturgy, they should sing alternately with the clergy or the choir, as it is prescribed. If this is done, then it will no longer happen that the people either make no answer at all to the public prayers – whether in the language of the Liturgy or in the vernacular – or at best utter the responses in a low and subdued manner. (*Divini Cultus* 18)

It is clear that Pope Pius XI understood the Mass as the work of the *whole* Church, not just her clergy. His call for the faithful to be "filled with a deep sense of the beauty of the Liturgy" is an ancestor of the later call to liturgical catechesis which makes that possible. That same year (1928), he had written an encyclical on the Sacred Heart of Jesus in which he spoke of the participation of all the faithful in the priesthood of Christ:

Nor do those only enjoy a participation in this mystic priesthood and in the office of satisfying and sacrificing, whom our Pontiff Christ Jesus uses as His ministers to offer up the clean oblation to God's Name in every place from the rising of the sun to the going down, but *the whole Christian people* rightly called by the Prince of the Apostles "a chosen generation, a kingly priesthood," ought to offer [sacrifices] for sins both for itself and for all mankind... (*Miserentissimus Redemptor* 9)

He wrote that the faithful join their own offerings to the Eucharist: "with this most august Eucharistic Sacrifice there ought to be joined an oblation both of the ministers *and of all the faithful*, so that they also may 'present themselves living sacrifices, holy, pleasing unto God.'" (*Ibid.*)

Pope Pius XII also wrote about the manner in which the faithful participate in the Mass in his 1947 encyclical on the liturgy (the first of its kind), *Mediator Dei* (MD).[3] He praised those who worked to make the faithful more familiar with the *Roman Missal* (the book from which the priest prays the Mass, up until recently called the *Sacramentary*) so that their participation in the Mass would be more fruitful; he also wrote favorably of the "dialogue Mass" which encouraged the faithful to speak or chant the responses of the Mass. (MD 105) He promoted several pious practices (e.g. praying the Rosary, visiting the Blessed Sacrament)

---

[3] Pope Pius XII outlined the four "ends" of Mass (which were listed at the beginning of the Introduction) in paragraphs 71-74 of *Mediator Dei*.

aimed at deepening the spiritual life of the faithful and preventing their participation in the liturgy from falling into "empty ritualism." (MD 175) Like his predecessor, Pope Pius XII directly connected the participation of the faithful in the liturgy with the common priesthood shared by all who are baptized into Christ. (cf. MD 88)

Avoiding "empty ritualism" is as important for the laity as it is for the clergy. The Constitution on the Sacred Liturgy made it clear that the faithful need to be properly disposed to be receptive to the liturgy, and that priests cannot expect this spiritual disposition to be brought about *only* by following the liturgical rubrics:

> But in order that the liturgy may be able to produce its full effects, it is *necessary that the faithful come to it with proper dispositions*, that their minds should be attuned to their voices, and that they should cooperate with divine grace lest they receive it in vain. Pastors of souls must therefore realize that, when the liturgy is celebrated, something *more is required than the mere observation of the laws* governing valid and licit celebration; it is their duty *also to ensure that the faithful take part fully aware* of what they are doing, actively engaged in the rite, and enriched by its effects. (CSL 11)

The Council was not downplaying the importance of observing liturgical laws, but was emphasizing that *in addition to* this obedience there must be a personal spiritual awareness that cannot simply be manufactured or mandated, but must be developed and nurtured, starting in baptism and continuing for the whole life of each Catholic.

This link between baptism and participation in the liturgy was repeated before, during, and after Vatican II. The 1958 instruction *De Musica Sacra* (DMS), the Constitution on the Sacred Liturgy, and the 1967 instruction *Musicam Sacram* (MS) all affirm that the laity "participate actively in the liturgy by virtue of their baptismal character" (DMS 93b) and that such participation is "their right and duty by reason of their baptism." (CSL 14; cf. MS 15) *Actual* participation, then, is only possible through baptism.

Pope John Paul II, in an address to Bishop of the United States in 1998, explained the three terms describing participation:

> *Full* participation certainly means that *every member of the community has a part* to play in the liturgy ... [but it] does not mean that everyone does everything, since this would lead to a clericalizing of the laity and a laicizing of the priesthood; and this was not what

the Council had in mind. The liturgy, like the Church, is intended to be hierarchical and polyphonic, respecting the different roles assigned by Christ and allowing all the different voices to blend in one great hymn of praise.

Active participation certainly means that, *in gesture, word, song and service*, all the members of the community take part in an act of worship … [but it] does not preclude the *active passivity* of silence, stillness and listening: indeed, it demands it. …

Conscious participation calls for the entire community to be *properly instructed* in the mysteries of the liturgy, lest the experience of worship degenerate into a form of *ritualism*. But it does not mean a constant attempt within the liturgy itself to *make the implicit explicit*, since this often leads to a verbosity and informality … [nor does it] mean that the Latin language, and especially the chants which are so superbly adapted to the genius of the Roman Rite, should be wholly abandoned.

Internal and External Participation

The 1958 instruction praised those faithful who used a personal missal which enabled them to better understand and more closely follow the prayers of the Mass. These personal missals helped the faithful unite *internal* participation with *external* participation. (cf. DMS 29) The internal aspect of participation "consists in paying devout attention," of achieving the proper internal disposition. This participation is more complete when it is joined to external acts (e.g. postures, gestures, "and especially responses, prayers, and singing"). The highest degree of participation is *sacramental* participation, achieved when the Catholic is properly disposed to receive Holy Communion. (cf. DMS 22)

The Second Vatican Council recognized in its Constitution on the Sacred Liturgy that active or actual participation is not merely a matter of external manifestation, but also of internal disposition. (cf. CSL 19) The distinction between internal and external participation was reiterated in the 1967 instruction:

This participation (a) should be above all internal, in the sense that by it *the faithful join their mind to what they pronounce or hear*, and cooperate with heavenly grace; (b) it must be, on the other hand, external also, that is, such as *to show the internal participation by gestures and bodily attitudes*, by the acclamations, responses and singing. The faithful should also be taught to *unite themselves interiorly to what the ministers or choir sing*, so that by listening to them they may raise their minds to God. (MS 15)

5

Because participation "should be above all internal," simply saying the responses and making the gestures (examples of *external* participation) without joining the mind to the actions is *not* "actual participation," since external participation must be a manifestation of internal participation.

Another component of internal participation is attentively *listening* to the prayers or chants, because a person need not be "doing something" (speaking or singing or moving) to be *active*. We live in a day and age which regards silence and stillness as merely the lull between one noise or action and the next. Joseph Cardinal Ratzinger (later elected as Pope Benedict XVI) wrote in his 2000 book *The Spirit of the Liturgy* that, after the Second Vatican Council, "active participation"

> was very quickly misunderstood to mean something external, entailing a need for general activity, as if as many people as possible, as often as possible, should be visibly engaged in action. However, the word "part-icipation" refers to a principal action in which everyone has a "part." And so if we want to discover the kind of doing that active participation involves, we need, first of all, to determine what this central *actio* is in which all the members of the community are supposed to participate. (p. 171)

Liturgical Catechesis

At Vatican II, the Church again recognized that this *authentic* participation in the liturgy does not come about without teaching the faithful about the liturgy and aiding them to cultivate the dispositions necessary for internal participation which leads to external participation. The necessity of liturgical catechesis – not only for the laity, but also for the clergy – was made clear in the same paragraph which identified participation as vital to the life of every Christian:

> [P]astors of souls must zealously strive to achieve it, by means of the *necessary instruction*, in all their pastoral work. Yet it would be futile to entertain any hopes of realizing this unless the pastors themselves, in the first place, become thoroughly imbued with the spirit and power of the liturgy, and undertake to give instruction about it. A *prime need*, therefore, is that attention be directed, first of all, to the *liturgical instruction of the clergy*. (CSL 14)

A few paragraphs later, the Constitution repeats the call to pastors to promote, "with zeal and patience ... the liturgical instruction of the faithful, and also their *active participation* in the liturgy both *internally* and *externally*." (CSL 19)

The contemporary Catechism defines the aim of liturgical catechesis as the initiation of people into the mystery of Christ "by proceeding from the visible to the invisible, from the sign to the thing signified, from the 'sacraments' to the 'mysteries.'" (*Catechism* 1075) This form of catechesis is called *mystagogy*. The term "mystagogical catechesis" has existed since the early centuries of the Church. In the late 4th century, St. Cyril of Jerusalem wrote several volumes of a mystagogical catechesis for new members of the Church.

Pope John Paul II wrote about this catechesis in his 2004 Apostolic Letter *Mane Nobiscum Domine* (MND) with which he inaugurated a "Year of the Eucharist":

> Pastors should be committed to that "mystagogical" catechesis so dear to the Fathers of the Church, by which the faithful are helped to *understand the meaning* of the liturgy's words and actions, to *pass from its signs to the mystery* which they contain, and to *enter into that mystery* in every aspect of their lives. (MND 17)

Pope Benedict XVI, in his Apostolic Exhortation following the 2005 Synod of Bishops on the Eucharist *Sacramentum Caritatis* (SC), addressed the need for *mystagogical* catechesis:

> [T]he Synod of Bishops asked that the faithful be helped to make their interior dispositions correspond to their gestures and words. Otherwise, however carefully planned and executed our liturgies may be, they would risk falling into a certain ritualism. ... The Synod Fathers unanimously indicated [a] mystagogical approach to catechesis, which would lead the faithful to understand more deeply the mysteries being celebrated. (SC 64)

He then outlined three key elements of mystagogical catechesis, echoing the three steps described earlier by his predecessor:

1) **interpreting** the liturgical rites in the light of salvation history
2) **explaining** the signs and symbols used in the rites
3) **relating** the rites to all the dimensions of Christian life.

The New Translation: A Sacral Vernacular

In 2001, the Congregation for Divine Worship and the Discipline of the Sacraments issued *Liturgiam Authenticam* (LA), a fifth instruction on the proper implementation of the Constitution on the Sacred Liturgy. It set forth the regulations by which translations of the Latin texts were to be made, after remarking that liturgical translations in certain places were in need of improvement:

> The omissions or errors which affect certain existing vernacular translations ... have impeded the progress of the inculturation that actually should have taken place. Consequently, the Church has been prevented from laying the foundation for a fuller, healthier and more authentic renewal. (LA 6)

The third typical edition of the *Roman Missal* was promulgated in Latin in 2002. This edition is substantially identical to the first edition published in 1970 and the second edition published in 1975. For the past several decades, Mass celebrated in English in the United States of America has used a 1973 translation of the 1970 Latin text. In late 2008, a new English translation of a portion of the 2002 edition of the *Roman Missal* was approved by the Holy See.[4] Now that the entirety of the new translation has been approved, it will be used wherever the Roman Rite is celebrated in English after a suitable period of catechesis; it is expected that the new translation will be in use by Easter or Advent of 2011.

The Church calls for a way of using the vernacular that sets it apart (consecrates it) for use in the liturgy and in prayer, "a kind of language which is easily understandable, yet which at the same times preserves [the] dignity, beauty, and doctrinal precision" of the prayers of the Church. (LA 25) This is described as "the development of a *sacral vernacular*, characterized by a vocabulary, syntax and grammar that are proper to divine worship." (LA 47) This language involves, at times, a sacred vocabulary (e.g. "chalice" instead of "cup"), the coining of new words, the use of transliteration (e.g. *consubstantialis* being translated as "consubstantial" rather than "one in being"), and a variety of expression which corresponds to the Latin (e.g. not starting every prayer with the same title for God, and not using the word "love" for both *caritas* and *dilectio*). Another notable feature is that since many of the liturgical texts are meant to be spoken aloud, they differ in style from texts meant to be read silently: some examples of this include "recurring patterns of syntax and style, a solemn or exalted tone, alliteration or assonance, concrete

---

[4] This portion, known as the "ordinary" or the "Order of Mass," makes up the unchanging structure of the Mass. The parts of Mass that change from one liturgical day to the next are called the "Propers." This book focuses on the Order of the Mass, not the Propers.

and vivid images, repetition, parallelism and contrast, a certain rhythm, and at times, the lyric of poetic compositions." (LA 59)

The new translation is more faithful to the Latin and the majority of the parts of the Mass spoken or chanted by the congregation has remained the same.[5] But the possibility of questions or confusion over the new texts is still there, especially concerning the *choice* of words. Just because a text is in a language you can *read* does not mean you can necessarily *understand* it. This is as true in the old translation as it is in the new translation. This is why the instruction also emphasized the need for catechesis to accompany the introduction of new translations:

> [I]f more significant changes are necessary … it will be preferable to make such changes at one time.… In such case, *a suitable period of catechesis should accompany the publication* of the new text. (LA 74)

> It is to be hoped that this new effort will provide stability in the life of the Church, so as to lay a firm foundation for supporting the liturgical life of God's people and *bringing about a solid renewal of catechesis*. (LA 133)

English and Latin

Praying the Mass includes the Latin words of the Mass along with the new English translation. How come?

There has been a common misconception since the 1970's that using Latin in the liturgy is a sign of "rolling back" or "cancelling" the liturgical reforms of the Second Vatican Council. But this is untrue for at least two important reasons. First, Latin is the language of the Roman (Latin) Rite of the Catholic Church, and the Second Vatican Council did not change that. Just months before the Council began, Bl. Pope John XXIII (who convoked the Council) wrote an Apostolic Constitution (*Veterum Sapientia*, "Wisdom of the Ancient World") praising the Latin language as universal, immutable, and non-vernacular, mandating its study, and affirming its retention in the Church.

Second, there has been a liturgical renewal brewing over the past several years, and part of that renewal has included the rediscovery of

---

[5] In both the old translation *and* the new translation, the words that the Church gives to us in the liturgy are the words which should be prayed. No one – whether lay, religious, or clergy – has the right to change, add, or omit words to these prayers. It is not permitted to change the words of a prayer to avoid, for example, using a masculine pronoun such as *He* or *Him* or the title *Father* when referring to God.

Latin and Gregorian chant even in the Ordinary Form of the Mass (the liturgy as revised following Vatican II). The Council, while permitting and welcoming the inclusion of the vernacular in the liturgy, also called for the retention of Latin and Gregorian chant:

> Particular law remaining in force, *the use of the Latin language is to be preserved* in the Latin rites. (CSL 36.1)

> [S]teps should be taken so that the faithful may also be able to *say or to sing together in Latin* those parts of the Ordinary of the Mass which pertain to them. (CSL 54)

> The Church acknowledges *Gregorian chant as specially suited to the Roman liturgy:* therefore, other things being equal, it should be given pride of place in liturgical services. (CSL 116)

These points have been reiterated by the Church over the years, but they have not always been heard and relayed. By providing the Latin and the English texts, this book will help you understand not only the words you say in English, but also the Latin you *might* say if you are ever at a Mass which incorporates Latin responses or chants.

Ordinary and Extraordinary

This book is about the *Ordinary Form of the Roman Rite*. This is a relatively new term to the Church. In July of 2007, Pope Benedict XVI issued an Apostolic Letter *motu proprio* (meaning "on his own impulse") entitled *Summorum Pontificum* which addressed issues concerning the older liturgy of the Roman Rite. This older form of the Mass has many names: the 1962 Missal, the Pian Missal (named after Pope Pius V), the Traditional Latin Mass, the Tridentine Mass, the pre-Vatican II Mass, the Gregorian Rite (named for Pope St. Gregory the Great), and so on. The newer form of the Mass also has many names: the 1970 Missal, the Pauline Missal (named after Pope Paul VI), the post-Vatican II Mass, the *Novus Ordo*, and so on. All of these titles vary in degree of accuracy.

In his Apostolic Letter, the Holy Father made it permissible for any priest of the Roman Rite to celebrate Mass according to the older form of the Mass, the liturgical books as they were published by Bl. Pope John XXIII in 1962.[6] He also provided simple and consistent language for us to use to speak of the older and newer liturgical forms:

---

[6] These liturgical books have since undergone slight revisions under Pope Benedict, so the term "1962 Missal" is no longer accurate.

The Roman Missal promulgated by Paul VI is the ordinary expression of the *Lex orandi* [that is, the "law of prayer"] of the Catholic Church of the Latin rite. Nonetheless, the Roman Missal promulgated by St. Pius V and reissued by Bl. John XXIII is to be considered as an extraordinary expression of that same *Lex orandi*, and must be given due honor for its venerable and ancient usage. These two *expressions* of the Church's *Lex orandi* will in no any way lead to a division in the Church's *Lex credendi* [that is, the "law of belief"]. They are, in fact two usages of the one Roman rite. (*Summorum Pontificum*, Article 1)

The one Roman Rite has two "usages" or "expressions" or "forms" – so the Church celebrates Mass in the *Ordinary Form* and the *Extraordinary Form*. This book is about the Ordinary Form of the Mass, although there are a few references to the Extraordinary Form.

Praying the Mass

What *is* "praying the Mass"? The Mass is made up of several prayers which take the form of responses, chants, and orations of varying length, but the Mass is *one* coherent, constant prayer. Rather than thinking that you are praying *at* Mass (and then, only when you are *saying* something), you should come to realize that everything you sing and say and do and see and hear and smell *is* one great prayer, the greatest prayer.

Praying the Mass was written to provide that mystagogical catechesis which Pope Benedict recognizes is needed in the Church today (and which has been in need since Vatican II, and even before then). This book is not intended to be a personal missal for use *during* Mass; it is, instead, a catechetical guide to the Mass. Its scope is intended to be universal – whether you are a bishop, priest, deacon, religious brother or sister, or lay Catholic, this book is meant to assist you in making the transition to the new English translation of the Mass. It is designed to help answer the questions "Why are we saying *this*?", "What does it *mean*?", and "What does it mean to *me*?" Where the translation has been changed, there is a mark in the margin on the left (») for quick visual recognition.

Hopefully, this catechesis will give you a greater understanding of the words in (English and Latin), postures, and gestures which make up the prayer of the Mass. You will learn the Scriptural origins for the various "movements" in this great symphony of prayer.[7] Each chapter begins with a verse from the Old Testament and a verse from the New Testament related to the part of the Mass being examined. Each chapter offers spiritual reflections to present the parts of the Mass to you in a new light. And each chapter ends with questions to lead you into further contemplation by **interpreting**, **explaining**, and **relating** the rites. The inexhaustible treasure trove of spiritual riches contained in the Mass will be opened more readily to you, and you can grow in holiness as the Church's liturgy takes on new meaning in your life and you begin to understand, to use the language of Cardinal Ratzinger, what is the *actio* in which we are called to participate.

The whole Mass is a prayer of worship and an encounter with the mystery of God. When you do more than just move your lips and your arms, when you *pray* the Mass, then you will be doing more than just "going to Mass," you will be worshiping God: you will learn how to "love the Lord your God with all your heart, and with all your soul, and with all your strength, and with all your mind." (Luke 10:27)

---

[7] Much of what is said in the Mass is contained nearly word-for-word in Scripture. The book of Revelation, in addition to containing many liturgical phrases used in the Mass, is also seen as a "blueprint" for the liturgical worship of the Church on earth participating in the eternal worship in Heaven. See the essay "The Mass and the Apocalypse" by Michael Barber, in *Catholic for a Reason III: Scripture and the Mystery of the Mass* (pp. 109-121), as well as Scott Hahn's excellent book, *The Lamb's Supper*.

Let my prayer be counted as incense before you,
and the lifting up of my hands as an evening sacrifice!
(Psalm 141:2)

"Watch and pray that you may not enter into temptation;
the spirit indeed is willing, but the flesh is weak."
(Matthew 26:41)

1

Preparing for Prayer

THE LIGHTS ARE dimmed, the popcorn is prepared, and the television volume is turned up (and then down). We sit on the couch with our feet up, and we put on a blanket if we're cold.

The car seat and mirrors are adjusted. The seatbelt is fastened. The radio stations (or CDs) are selected. The trip odometer is reset to zero.

We prepare for watching a movie or for taking a long car trip. If the lights are too bright, the volume is too low, our head touches the ceiling of the car, or all we hear is static, we have let obstacles get in the way of what we intended to do. Why would prayer be any different?

Whether it is personal or communal, liturgical or extemporaneous, prayer requires us to have the right disposition for it to be fruitful. The Church calls us to prepare ourselves for the prayer of the Mass in various ways, some of which are obligatory.

Personal Prayer

At the Second Vatican Council, the Church confirmed *five times* that the Eucharistic liturgy is both the source and summit of the activity of the Church, and therefore of each of her members:

[T]he liturgy is the *summit* toward which the activity of the Church is directed; at the same time it is the *font* from which all her power flows. (CSL 10)

Taking part in the Eucharistic sacrifice, which is the *fount* and *apex* of the whole Christian life, they offer the Divine Victim to God, and offer themselves along with It. (*Lumen Gentium* 11)

[P]astors should see to it that the celebration of the Eucharistic Sacrifice is the *center* and *culmination* of the whole life of the Christian community. (*Christus Dominus* 30.2)

[T]he Eucharist shows itself as the *source* and the *apex* of the whole work of preaching the Gospel. (*Presbyterorum Ordinis* 5)

By the preaching of the word and by the celebration of the sacraments, the *center* and *summit* of which is the most holy Eucharist, He brings about the presence of Christ, the author of salvation. (*Ad Gentes* 9)

The Eucharist is the ultimate aim (but not the *only* aim) of life in Christ: communion with God and His Church in Holy Communion. It is also the primary source (but not the *only* source) of that Christian life. During the years following Vatican II, there seems to have been a misconception that going to Mass once a week was *all* a Catholic should need. But the Council said exactly the *opposite*, that although the Eucharist is the source and summit, the spiritual life

is *not* limited solely to participation in the liturgy. The Christian is indeed called to pray with his brethren, but he must also enter into his chamber to *pray to the Father, in secret*; yet more, according to the teaching of the Apostle [Paul], he should *pray without ceasing*. We learn from the same Apostle that we must always *bear about in our body the dying of Jesus*,[1] so that the life also of Jesus may be made manifest in our bodily frame. (CSL 12)

That quote from the Constitution on the Liturgy was referring to *your* **personal prayer life**. Another document from the Council relates those same aspects of the spiritual life to the laity:

[The laity] should all remember that they can reach all men and contribute to the salvation of the whole world by *public worship* and *prayer* as well as by *penance* and voluntary acceptance of the labors and hardships of life whereby they become like the suffering Christ. (*Apostolicam Actuositatem* 16)

---

[1] This is probably a reference to mortification, that is, practicing self-discipline and penance to overcome sinful tendencies and grow in virtue. See page 21 for an example.

Devout participation in the Mass gives life to your personal prayer, and by nurturing your prayer life, your participation in the Mass becomes deeper and more fruitful. A deeply personal life of *prayer* is the key to an immensely fruitful life of *faith*. The Church describes the necessity of an intimate relationship with Christ in these words from Vatican II:

> [T]he success of the lay apostolate depends upon *the laity's living union with Christ*, in keeping with the Lord's words, "He who abides in me, and I in him, bears much fruit, for without me you can do nothing" (John 15:5). This *life of intimate union with Christ* in the Church is nourished by spiritual aids which are common to all the faithful, *especially active participation in the sacred liturgy.* ... In this way the laity must *make progress in holiness* in a happy and ready spirit, trying prudently and patiently to overcome difficulties. (*Apostolicam Actuositatem* 4)

If you don't have a "life of intimate union with Christ," then the seed of the Eucharist ends up on "the path" or on "rocky ground" where it will not bear fruit. (Matt. 13:4-5) Prayer is the door to that union with Christ; it is "the raising of one's mind and heart to God." (*Catechism* 2559)

"Warming up"

The liturgy (and in particular the Mass) is the "corporate" worship of the Church. The word "corporate" might make you think of businesses and companies and corporations, but it comes from the Latin *corporare* which means "to form into a body." The word means "pertaining to a body," and since the Church is the *Body* of Christ (of which you are a member), it makes sense that the public, official worship of the Church is her *corporate* worship.

Just as when engaging in *full-body* exercise, you need to warm up by stretching *individual* muscle groups, each member of the Body of Christ needs to engage in a similar discipline to prepare for *corporate* prayer: "warming up" with *personal* prayer. This can be done at home or at your church, although you can pray anywhere, anytime. Prayer can be vocal, meditative, or contemplative. (cf. *Catechism* 2720-2724) The Church also recommends devotional prayer, such as the Stations of the Cross, the Rosary, the Chaplet of Divine Mercy, and novenas and litanies. A most excellent form of prayer is Eucharistic Adoration, time spent in prayer in the presence of the Blessed Sacrament either reserved in the tabernacle or exposed in a monstrance. The Church encourages these devotional forms of prayer because they harmonize with the liturgical seasons, are shaped by the liturgy, and lead us back to the liturgy itself. (cf. CSL 13)

However and whatever and wherever you pray, *just pray!* Build a habit of daily prayer. If you don't warm up before exercising, your body will not react properly (and you might injure yourself). If you don't "warm up" before the prayer of the Mass, you might find yourself too easily distracted by things going on around you. If you find that your mind often wanders during Mass, you may want to pray before Mass for greater concentration. Consider praying to your guardian angel for assistance: because the Mass is a participation in the heavenly liturgy, all the angels of Heaven, including your guardian angel, are present at every celebration of the Eucharist. Ask your angel to help you stay focused on the spiritual realities present at the Mass, especially the mystery of faith, the miraculous change of the bread and wine into the Eucharist.

Reading the Bible

Along with the Church's liturgy (and even everyday life) the Bible is a "wellspring" of prayer because it gives us "surpassing knowledge of Jesus Christ." (*Catechism* 2652-2653; Phil. 3:8) Reading the Bible is an excellent way to pray, and reading it *regularly* will help you form a habit of prayer.

One of the benefits of a liturgical calendar is that the readings for any given day are determined ahead of time (except in a few cases where there is a choice of readings). This means that you can **become familiar with the Scripture you are going to hear** by reading it yourself. In his response to the Synod of Bishops on the Eucharist, Pope Benedict wrote that the celebration of the Mass

> is enhanced when priests and liturgical leaders are committed to making known the current liturgical texts and norms, making available the great riches found in the General Instruction of the Roman Missal and the Order of Readings for Mass. Perhaps we take it for granted that our ecclesial communities already know and appreciate these resources, but this is not always the case. These texts contain riches which have preserved and expressed the faith and experience of the People of God over its two-thousand-year history. (SC 40)

He draws attention specifically to the Order of Readings for Mass, thus expressing a desire that the faithful would become better acquainted with the Scripture they will be hearing at Mass. Some parish bulletins include the Scripture citations for the coming week. Some Catholic bibles have an appendix with the readings listed for the Sundays and feast days of the year. You can use the USCCB web site's calendar to pull up a digital version of the readings for the day. [2]

Some parishes provide missalettes with the Sunday readings in them, or perhaps you have a private daily missal or a periodical like *Magnificat*; if this is the case, you can come to Mass a few minutes earlier than usual and spend some private time with the Word of God. Some parishes hold Bible studies which look at the coming Sunday's readings. There are also free resources on the Internet which provide meditations and reflections on the readings at Mass; three such web sites are "The Word Among Us" (www.wau.org), "Mobile Gabriel" (www.mobilegabriel.com), and the Passionists' web site (www.passionist.org).

Although such preparation is not *required*, it can help you pay closer attention when the readings are proclaimed at Mass. We only hear them read once, and if we become distracted for some reason, we might miss an important word or verse (and they're *all* important words). But if you read them ahead of time, you can read them as many times as you want, as slowly as you like, and meditate on them without missing anything.

This practice is even more strongly recommended for families. The home is the "domestic church," the primary place where children are to learn – by the example of their parents – to encounter Christ on a daily basis. This includes introducing them to the liturgical life of the Church. Try to find the time during the week to sit down together to read the Scriptures for the upcoming Sunday Mass and discuss them.

Even if you only go to Mass on Sundays, daily reading of Scripture (whether from the Mass readings or not) is a way to keep your prayer life going. For example, if you are having trouble thinking of things to say to God in prayer, try praying the Psalms. The Church does this as one body through the **Liturgy of the Hours** (or **Divine Office**), by which the Church sanctifies the hours of the day, dedicating them to God, through prayer. Priests and religious pray the Liturgy of the Hours as part of their vocation, and many laypeople pray it as a private devotion as well; the

---

[2] The USCCB calendar of readings is at *http://www.usccb.org/nab/*.

Church even encourages the praying of the Liturgy of the Hours as a parish family on Sundays and feast days. (cf. *CSL* 100)

Daily reading of Scripture is so important because of *what* the Bible *is*. Imagine you receive a love letter from your spouse. Your spouse's love for you is why he or she *wrote* the letter; your love for your spouse is why you should *read* the letter! The Bible is God's love letter to mankind, and to each one of us individually; in its pages we learn Who God is, what He has done for us, and what He is doing in our lives even now! The Scriptures are so important to the Christian life that St. Jerome wrote, in the early 5th century, that

> if, according to the apostle Paul, Christ is "the power of God and the wisdom of God" (1 Cor. 1:24) and who does not know Scripture does not know the power or the wisdom of God, then *ignorance of Scripture is ignorance of Christ*. (Introduction to Isaiah)

If we are going to be in conversation with God, we should give Him a chance to speak: in prayer, we speak to God, and in reading Scripture, He speaks to us. (cf. *Catechism* 2653)

The Eucharistic Fast

In the past few decades, the Church has changed her discipline regarding the fast before receiving Holy Communion. At one time, Catholics were required to abstain from all food and drink from midnight if they were going to receive Communion that day. The fast was reduced to three hours in 1957 by Pope Pius XII. The current discipline established by Pope Paul VI in 1964 requires all who are healthy enough to do so to **fast for one hour before reception of Communion** (not one hour before *Mass*) from all food and drink, with the exception of water and medicine. (cf. *Code of Canon Law*, 919) For those who can, I recommend fasting for longer than an hour. Why? Read on.

Why do we fast before receiving Communion? In St. Paul's first letter to the Corinthians, he admonished some of them for eating and drinking (and getting drunk!) when they assembled for worship, while others were going hungry. (cf. 1 Cor. 11:20-21) Avoiding normal food before receiving Communion helps to remind us just what it is we are receiving in this sacrament, and to approach the Eucharist with proper reverence. St. Justin Martyr, writing to the Roman Emperor Augustus

Caesar in the 2nd century, explained that "not as common bread and common drink do we receive" the Eucharist, but that it is "the flesh and blood of that Jesus who was made flesh." (Apology I, 66)

Fasting is also a traditional Christian mortification (a discipline of bodily self-denial). Mortifications serve to subject our bodily desires to our spiritual needs. St. Paul wrote to the Corinthians "I pommel my body and subdue it," because he was aware that his bodily urges could jeopardize his spiritual well-being. (1 Cor. 9:27) Fasting was practiced by numerous figures in the Bible – such as Moses, Elijah, and Jesus – to prepare themselves for what was to come. By putting aside our corporal need for food and drink – especially if we fast for *more* than just an hour before receiving Communion – we can use our bodies' natural reaction of hunger to stir up in our souls the *spiritual* hunger we should have for our spiritual food, the Body and Blood of our Lord. We fast while we wait for Jesus, the bridegroom, and that fast ends when we receive the bridegroom in Holy Communion. (cf. Luke 5:34-35)

Sacramental Confession

It is important to **be in a state of grace** when you present yourself to receive Holy Communion. (cf. *Catechism* 1415) This means you are not aware of having committed a mortal sin since your last Confession. If you *are* aware of having sinned mortally, it is imperative (for the good of your soul, and possibly others') to receive absolution in the sacrament of Reconciliation before receiving Communion. (cf. *Catechism* 1385) The words of St. Paul to the Corinthians explain why:

> Whoever, therefore, eats the bread or drinks the cup of the Lord in an unworthy manner will be guilty of profaning the body and blood of the Lord. Let a man examine himself, and so eat of the bread and drink of the cup. For any one who eats and drinks without discerning the body eats and drinks judgment upon himself. (1 Cor. 11:27-29)

The Church echoes St. Paul's concern for our spiritual (and eternal) well-being.

Although Confession is only *necessary* in the case of mortal sin, it is strongly recommended that you make a regular practice of Confession of venial sins, because the graces you receive in that sacrament give you "an increase of spiritual strength for the Christian battle." (*Catechism* 1496)

Silence and Stillness

Do you listen to the radio as you drive to work? Do you listen to music on an iPod as you run? Do you turn the television on as soon as you get home? Many of us live with constant background noise; silence is seen as a void waiting to be filled. When was the last time you sat still for an hour or two? Maybe it was while watching a movie or otherwise being entertained.

Silence and stillness are not burdens to be endured but treasures to be sought after. The "still small voice" (1 Kgs. 19:12) of God can often be drowned out by the constant noise and activity of the world. Jesus surely hears the prayers we express in the silent sanctuaries of our hearts (cf. *Catechism* 2616), and it is in "this silence, unbearable to the 'outer' man, [that] the Father speaks to us His incarnate Word." (*Catechism* 2717) In contemplative or meditative prayer, the words of the psalmist ring true, "For God alone my soul waits *in silence*" (Ps. 62:1), and the words of God come in reply: "*Be still* and know that I am God." (Ps. 46:10)

During the Mass, there are periods of silence – not just silence on the part of the congregation while the priest or someone else speaks or sings, but total silence among all those present. It can be difficult, or even uncomfortable, to people who are used to constant action and ambient noise. Just as uncomfortable is stillness, whether standing or sitting or kneeling. We might often think "Did someone forget what to do?" or "What is the priest waiting for?"

Rarely do we think to ask ourselves in this silence and stillness, "Whose presence am I in? What am *I* doing?" God's transcendence and majesty should give us pause: "The LORD is in his holy temple; let all the earth keep silence before him." (Hab. 2:20) Spend time before Mass in silence contemplating these things, and when there is silence during the Mass, put it to good use.

Having prepared yourself for the Mass with fasting and prayer – putting off the shoes from your feet, as did Moses – you are ready to follow our Lord Jesus Christ in His prayer to the Father. But if you are going to follow Him, you must be willing to take up your cross. (cf. Matt. 16:24)

Questions for Reflection

1) **Interpret:** Consider the words of the Our Father: "give us this day our daily bread." How can your body's physical reaction to fasting inform you of your spiritual dependence on God for all your needs, both spiritual and physical?

2) **Interpret:** Right before Communion, we say that we are not worthy, but how can we receive Holy Communion *worthily*?

3) **Explain:** How is the sanctuary of the church prepared for Mass? Why are candles lit? Why is there a crucifix on or near the altar? Why are different liturgical days associated with specific colors?

4) **Explain:** After fasting in the desert for forty days, Jesus quoted Deuteronomy 8:3 to rebuke Satan, saying "Man shall not live by bread alone, but by *every word* that proceeds from the mouth of God." (Matt. 4:4) Why is so much importance given to the Bible in the formation of a healthy prayer life?

5) **Relate:** How much time do you spend reading the Bible? How can private or communal reading of Scripture help you to better understand the readings you hear at Mass?

6) **Relate:** What sorts of things do you pray for? How much time do you spend in prayers of *contrition* and *petition*? Do you spend as much time in prayers of *thanksgiving* and *adoration* of God for the things He has done for you?

7) **Relate:** How do you spend your time *right before* you go to Mass? Are you attuning your mind to the sacred or are you clinging to the secular? Are you preparing yourself to encounter the mystery of God?

"Go through the city, through Jerusalem, and put a mark upon the foreheads of the men who sigh and groan over all the abominations that are committed in it."
(Ezekiel 9:4)

Then I saw another angel ascend from the rising of the sun, with the seal of the living God ... saying, "Do not harm the earth or the sea or the trees, till we have sealed the servants of our God upon their foreheads."
(Revelation 7:2-3)

2

Sign of the Cross

I HAVE BEEN TO numerous Catholic retreats and conferences and lectures. On more than one occasion, the speaker, faced with a room of people talking and milling about, has gotten their attention in under two seconds with six simple words: "In the name of the Father..." Upon hearing those words, everybody stops what they are doing and makes the Sign of the Cross. Some might call it conditioning, but Catholics recognize the sacredness and solemnity of the Sign of the Cross.

In nómine Patris, et Fílii, et Spíritus Sancti.

In the name of the Father, and of the Son,   *Matt. 28:19*
and of the Holy Spirit.

After the Introit or entrance hymn has ended and the priest stands at his chair, he "gets our attention" with these powerful words. Along with these words, taken from the lips of Christ himself, we bow our heads and trace a cross, from head to torso, from left shoulder to right shoulder. We might have already made this gesture with holy water upon entering the church, as a reminder of our baptism.

The Words

Let us first concentrate on the words spoken by the priest. (This book is focused on the words spoken by the laity, but because we all say these words so often, we should take the time to study them. These words should begin and end every prayer we offer.)

We believe that God is a Holy Trinity, three Divine Persons in one God: Father, Son, and Holy Spirit. When we pray the Sign of the Cross, we confess that God has *one* name: "In *the* name of the Father, *and* of the Son, *and* of the Holy Spirit." Not "names" but "name."

God revealed His name to Moses when He commissioned him to go to Egypt and be His instrument of liberation for His people Israel. God tells Moses that he is to "say this to the sons of Israel, 'I AM has sent me to you.'" (Ex. 3:14) The revealed *covenant* name of God is *Yahweh*[1] (often represented by the letters *YHWH*) which means "I AM WHO AM." In this Name, God reveals that He is the origin and principle of life, of existence, of being.

After God reveals this name to His people, we find that many of the prophets and priests and kings of Israel receive a name that refers to this revealed covenant name of God. The prophet Isaiah relayed so many striking prophecies of Christ and His Passion; his name means "salvation [is] of *Yah*[weh]" ("Isa*iah*"). Jeremiah prophesied the restoration of Israel by means of a new covenant with God; his name means "*Yah*[weh] will raise" ("Jerem*iah*"). During a time when Israel was divided in two and the people worshiped false gods, Elijah came to King Ahab and revealed by many miracles that *Yahweh* is the true God, not just of Israel but of all nations and all men; his name means "*Yah*[weh] is God" (Eli*jah*).

So it should come as no surprise to us that when Mary and Joseph were told of the impending birth of the Son of God, they were told that the name the child was to be given was already decided for them from before the foundation of the world: "You shall call his name Jesus, for he will save his people from their sins." (Matt. 1:21; cf. Luke 1:31)

---

[1] The use of the Divine Name *Yahweh* is not permitted during the liturgy; the word *Lord* should be used instead. The Divine Name was not spoken aloud in Israel's worship (substituting *Adonai* instead), and the first Christians (Jews and Greeks alike) used the Greek word *Kyrios* instead of the Divine Name. The tradition of the Church has been to avoid speaking the Divine Name aloud. (cf. *Letter to the Bishops' Conferences on "The Name of God"*, dated 29 June 2008, Prot. N. 213/08/L)

Where is the name *Yahweh* in "Jesus"? The English spelling "Jesus" comes to us from the Latin *Iesus*, which came from the Greek *Iesous*, which came from the Hebrew *Yehoshua* (or the Aramaic *Yeshua*). This name means "*Yah*[weh] saves" (*Ye*hoshua). The very name that the Son of God is given at His Incarnation is "God saves," and the angel tells Joseph that this child will grow up to "save *his* people from their sins." The angel is affirming the age-old Christian truth: Jesus is God!

There is another name (or title) that the Jews would use for God. To avoid profaning His name, they would substitute the word *Adonai* for *Yahweh*. The word *Adonai* translated into Greek is *Kyrios*; in Latin, it's *Dominus*; in English, "Lord." The early Church recognized the divinity of Jesus, not only by His birth-name, but by the title used to address Him. St. Paul records this eloquently in what might be an early Christian hymn:

> Therefore God has highly exalted him and *bestowed on him the name which is above every name*, that at the name of Jesus every knee should bow, in heaven and on earth and under the earth, and every tongue confess that *Jesus Christ is Lord*, to the glory of God the Father. (Phil. 2:9-11)

In Philippians 2:10-11, Paul reads the Old Testament in the light of the revelation of Jesus Christ: "I am God, and there is no other. ... 'To me every knee shall bow, every tongue shall swear.'" (Isa. 45:22-23) As St. Augustine wrote, the New Testament is concealed in the Old, and the Old Testament is revealed in the New. In the early Church, then, there was no divided allegiance between serving *the Lord* and serving *God*. The title of "Lord" was given by Israel to God (the Father) in the Old Testament and the Church retained that use while also recognizing it to be the rightful title of the Son as well; they also confessed that "the Lord is the Spirit." (2 Cor. 3:17)

While the name Jesus is proper to the Son alone, it is truly the name of God, because it reveals to us not only *Who* God is – "I AM WHO AM" – but also *what* God does: "God saves." The names of the Blessed Trinity – Father, Son, and Holy Spirit – describe their eternal relationship to one another even before creation. But Jesus reveals to us through His own name, and through His revelation of God as *Abba* ("Papa" or "Dad"), that God desires an everlasting relationship with us.

The words of the Sign of the Cross fulfill the words of St. Paul to the Corinthians: "We preach Christ crucified... Christ the power of God and the wisdom of God." (1 Cor. 1:23-24)

The Gesture

As the priest says these words, we spiritually fulfill the command of Jesus Christ to take up our crosses and follow Him. We bow our heads as a sign of reverence at the invocation of the Trinity (cf. GIRM 275a), and we draw the cross of the Lord from our head to the bottom of our chest, from our left shoulder to our right. (cf. *Catechism* 2157) In the *Eastern* Churches, the gesture goes from the right shoulder to the left. In the 13th century, Pope Innocent III explained the symbolism of the direction:

> From above to below, and from the right to the left, because Christ descended from the heavens to the earth, and from the Jews [right] He passed to the Gentiles [left]. Others, however, make the sign of the cross from the left to the right, because from misery [left] we must cross over to glory [right], just as Christ crossed over from death to life, and from Hades to Paradise.

It appears that moving from the right to the left was the ancient practice, and that the faithful began mirroring the way the priests made the sign when facing the people to bless them.

The cross is not a uniquely Christian symbol, and the shape of the cross has changed over time. In the book of the prophet Ezekiel, God tells a certain man to walk through Jerusalem and "put a *mark* upon the foreheads of the men who sign and groan" over the sins committed in it; this mark protected them from the punishment God would bring on the city. The word "mark" is the Hebrew letter *Tav*, the last letter of their alphabet. The ancient shape of this letter was a cross (T or + or X), and this sign was used in Ezekiel 9 as a seal of God's ownership. This sign was taken up by the Church; it may in fact be the seal seen by St. John in the book of Revelation:

> Then I saw another angel ascend from the rising of the sun, with the seal of the living God, and he called with a loud voice to the four angels who had been given power to harm earth and sea, saying, "Do not harm the earth or the sea or the trees, till we have sealed the servants of our God upon their foreheads." (Rev. 7:2-3)

Cardinal Ratzinger sees in this passage from Revelation "the meaning of this mysterious sign" in Ezekiel's vision "unveiled" in the light of the

Crucifixion. (*The Spirit of the Liturgy*, pp. 179-180; cf. 2 Cor. 3:15-17) The cross of Christ is "the seal of the living God" which identifies us as His people.[2]

The Sign of the Cross is rich with symbolism. It is the sign of the sacrifice of Christ, the price of our redemption, a manifestation of the love that God had for us, that "while we were yet sinners Christ died for us." (Rom. 5:8) It professes our faith in the Trinity, a God Who does not exist in isolation but in eternal communion, even before He created anything. Because we are created in the image of this Triune God, we too are created to exist in communion with one another and with God our Creator. This orients us toward self-sacrifice in imitation of Christ. (cf. Eph. 5:1-2) This orientation reminds us that, as Jesus paid with His life to give us the gift of the Mass, so we too pay with our lives: we are called to die to self, in our baptism and every day of our lives. As St. Paul wrote, "we know that our former man was crucified with him." (Rom. 6:6; cf. Gal. 2:20)

The Sign of the Cross always orients us to God, no matter what our situation. We make it in so many situations:

> We make the Sign of the Cross before we pray to collect and compose ourselves and to fix our minds and hearts and wills upon God. We make it when we finish praying in order that we may hold fast the gift we have received from God. In temptations we sign ourselves to be strengthened; in dangers, to be protected. The cross is signed upon us in blessings in order that the fullness of God's life may flow into the soul and fructify and sanctify us wholly. (Rev. Romano Guardini, *Sacred Signs*)

Tracing the Cross upon yourself

In the early Church, it was customary to trace the Sign of the Cross upon the forehead (as the book of Revelation suggests). Over time, the Sign began to be made over the whole upper body.

Head. God commanded Israel to consecrate priests, prophets, and kings to Him by anointing them on the forehead with oil. We enter into this three-fold office of Christ — as priest, prophet, and king — in our Baptism: after we are washed in the water, we are anointed on the head with oil. As you touch your forehead in the Sign of the Cross, remember

---

[2] This seal is also associated with the name of the Lamb and of the Father. (cf. Rev. 14:1; 22:4)

the anointing you received in your Baptism. Ask God to sanctify your mind and your thoughts.

As your hand moves from your forehead down to your chest, it passes your sensory organs: your eyes, your ears, your nose, and your mouth. With these organs you perceive the revelation of God in nature and in faith. Your whole body has been redeemed by the Cross.

Torso. God is all-knowing and sees into the very depths of our souls. We read in Scripture that "God is witness of [our] inmost feelings, and a true observer of [the] heart." (Wis. 1:6) "Search me, O God, and know my heart!" (Ps. 139:23) The love of God, manifested for us on the Cross, reaches into our deepest inner self. As your hand passes your heart and you touch the bottom of your chest in the Sign of the Cross, you form the vertical beam of the Cross, planting it in your inmost being. Ask God to sanctify your will and your emotions.

Shoulders. God liberated Israel from the yoke of slavery they endured in Egypt. The Exodus of the Israelites foreshadowed the Exodus (cf. Luke 9:30-31) on which Christ leads us by His crucifixion: "For freedom Christ has set us free; stand fast therefore, and do not submit again to a yoke of slavery." (Gal. 5:1) Christ frees us from the yoke of sin and offers us His own in return: "Take my yoke upon you, and learn from me; for I am gentle and lowly in heart, and you will find rest for your souls. For my yoke is easy, and my burden is light." (Matt. 11:29-30) A yoke is a beam that attaches two animals (often oxen) together to allow them to pull a load, such as a plow. A yoke is never carried alone: we are either yoked to Satan by sin, or we are yoked to Christ by the Cross. As you move your hand from one shoulder to the next in the Sign of the Cross, realize that you are taking the yoke of the Cross upon your shoulders, and that Christ joins himself to you by it. Ask God to sanctify your strength.

You trace upon your body the Cross on which hung the salvation of the world. As the body of Christ hung on the Cross for you, now you willingly take up that cross upon your own body.

Praying with your fingers

In addition to the prayerful action of tracing the cross, there is a hidden prayer in your own fingers. You may have noticed the way the hand of a priest is formed when he makes the Sign of the Cross over the bread and wine in the Eucharistic Prayer, or over the congregation at the blessing at the end of the Mass.

In the time of Pope Innocent III, priests were instructed to make the Sign of the Cross "with three fingers, because the signing is done together with the invocation of the Trinity." The first three fingers – the thumb, index finger, and middle finger – are held together as a symbol of the unity of the Trinity, three Persons in one God. The other two fingers are curled into the palm, symbolizing the descent of Christ from Heaven to earth and the unity of His two natures, divine and human.

Another way to hold the hand is to keep all five fingers together, signifying the five wounds Christ received during the crucifixion (His two hands, His two feet, and His side). A pious practice observed by some people is, after having made the Sign of the Cross, they place their thumb over their index finger (curling the other three fingers into their palm) thus making a small cross, which they kiss.

However you hold your hand, whatever you call to mind as you make the Sign of the Cross, make it slowly and deliberately. Make it a prayer which encompasses your whole person, body and soul.

Because the gesture of the Sign of the Cross is a testimony to both the Passion and the Resurrection, and the words of the prayer contain a confession of faith in the Trinity, "in the sign of the Cross, together with the invocation of the Trinity, the whole essence of Christianity is summed up." (*The Spirit of the Liturgy*, p. 178) To this powerful summary of the faith, what can we say in response but *Amen*?

Questions for Reflection

1) **Interpret:** *What* are we doing "In the name of the Father…"?
2) **Explain:** What does the Cross signify?
3) **Relate:** How do you make the Sign of the Cross? Does it have a special significance?
4) **Relate:** When else do you make the Sign of the Cross? Why?
5) **Relate:** How does the Cross remind us of the Church's mission?

Ezra blessed the LORD, *the great God;*
and all the people answered, "Amen, Amen."
(Nehemiah 8:6)

All the promises of God find their Yes *in Jesus Christ.*
That is why we utter the Amen *through him, to the glory of God.*
(2 Corinthians 1:20)

3

Common Responses and Postures

THE PEW IS A rather recent addition to Christian worship. Following the Protestant Reformation in the 16th century, which placed an emphasis on the pulpit and the sermon (rather than on the altar and the Eucharist), permanent seating gained popularity in churches. If you have attended an Eastern Divine Liturgy, you might have noticed that the faithful rarely sit down, or perhaps that there weren't even pews at all! For more than a millennium, Catholic worship was primarily carried out standing and kneeling. Nowadays, at any given Mass in the Roman Rite, we genuflect, sit, stand, and kneel. We also bow our heads or our bodies. These external bodily gestures manifest our internal spiritual dispositions: reverence, penitence, respect, awe.

This bodily participation is fondly called, in some places, "Catholic calisthenics," but I doubt this is what St. Paul had in mind when he wrote "*work out* your own salvation in fear and trembling." (Phil. 2:12)

"Amen."

The word *Amen* appears in the Old Testament around 30 times, and in the New Testament nearly 150 times. It is sometimes translated as "So be it" in the Old Testament, but usually it is left as *Amen*. In the gospels, it is only heard on the lips of Jesus; it is usually translated as "Amen, I say to you…" or "Truly, I say to you…" In St. John's Gospel, the word is found 50 times, always in pairs: each time Jesus uses the word, He says it twice for emphasis, "Amen, amen, I say to you…" Elsewhere in the New Testament, is it used almost exclusively as a word of prayer at the end of a sentence.

This word comes to us directly from Hebrew. The word *Amen* denotes agreement, assurance, consent, trust, and belief. When Jesus says "Amen, Amen," He assures us that what He is saying is true and worthy of our attention. When we say "Amen," we are giving our assent to the prayer that has been said; we are saying "I believe" and "I concur." Some recent scholarship has suggested that "Amen" is a nomadic word roughly meaning, "I'd hammer my tent-peg into that." A tent-peg is not secure in loose sand, but in solid ground. "Amen" is a statement of complete dependence and reliance. For this reason, it is important to *listen* to the prayers so that your assent is not an empty one. Saying "Amen" is a *personal act of faith*.

Writing to the church in Corinth, St. Paul defends Jesus as the truth: "For the Son of God, Jesus Christ, whom we preached among you … was not *Yes* and *No*; but in him it is always *Yes*. For all the promises of God find their *Yes* in him. That is why we utter the *Amen* through him, to the glory of God." (2 Cor. 1:19-21) This is why most of our prayers end with "through Christ our Lord, amen."

The only place the word *Amen* is not used as a word of prayer is in the mysterious book of the Revelation to St. John. John has a vision of the Lord Jesus, Who tells him to write messages to seven churches. To the seventh church, in Laodicea, Jesus begins His message with these words: "The words of the *Amen*, the faithful and true witness, the beginning of God's creation." (Rev. 3:14) Jesus takes *Amen* as a name, calling Himself faithful and true, because He cannot speak anything other than the truth, because He *is* the Truth. (cf. John 14:6)

"And with your spirit."

Another common response is made five times during the Mass: after the priest's greeting at the beginning of Mass, right before the Gospel is read, during the Preface of the Eucharistic Prayer, at the Sign of Peace, and right before the final blessing. The old English translation of the Mass rendered it as "And also with you," but the new translation properly conveys the true sense of this response:

Et cum spíritu tuo.

» And with your spirit.   *Gal. 6:18; 2 Tim. 4:22*

When the priest says "The Lord be with you," he is *not* simply saying the religious equivalent of a secular "Good morning" or "How are you?" Our response, then, cannot be misunderstood as a "You too." This greeting from the ordained minister and our response to him say more than any secular greeting or exchange of pleasantries can; the proper liturgical greeting also grounds the celebration of Mass firmly in the business of Heaven (the presence and power of God) rather than the business of earth (the weather and our personal dispositions). These words connect us to the sacred act we are participating in, drawing us out of our common worldly surroundings.

Why "your spirit" instead of "you"?[1] This question was addressed in 2006 by Francis Cardinal George, OMI, Archbishop of Chicago and current president of the United States Conference of Catholic Bishops:

> Our current translation might seem more personal and friendly, but that's the problem. The spirit referred to in the Latin is the spirit of Christ that comes to a priest when he is ordained, as St. Paul explained to St. Timothy. In other words, the people are saying in their response that Christ as head of the Church is the head of the liturgical assembly, no matter who the particular priest celebrant might be. That is a statement of faith, a statement distorted by transforming it into an exchange of personal greetings.

Why does the priest say "The Lord *be* with you" rather than "The Lord *is* with you"? Twice in Scripture, an angel appears to someone with the greeting, "The Lord *is* with you." (Judg. 6:12; Luke 1:28) These angels were delivering a message from God Himself. But there are also times in Scripture when a *man* says "The Lord is with you" and he turns

---

[1] "English is the only major language of the Roman Rite which did not translate the word *spiritu*. The Italian (*E con il tuo spirito*), French (*Et avec votre esprit*), Spanish (*Y con tu espíritu*) and German (*Und mit deinem Geiste*) renderings of 1970 all translated the Latin word *spiritu* precisely." (USCCB Bishops' Committee on the Liturgy Newsletter, vol. XLI)

out to be wrong! One such example is Nathan, a prophet during the reign of King David. (cf. 2 Sam. 7:3-4)

In the New Testament, only the Mother of the Lord is told that the Lord *is* with her; every other time the phrase is used (by St. Paul in his letters), he writes it as a prayer: "The Lord *be* with you." The difference is that whereas the angel Gabriel had it on the highest authority (God) that the Lord was truly with the Blessed Virgin, St. Paul offers a prayer that the Lord be with his fellow Christians, rather than simply *presume* that He was. Therefore, the priest at Mass begs God for His presence with His people, and the faithful respond with the same prayer in mind.

Standing

As mentioned previously, standing is the "classic" posture for prayer, inherited from the Jewish tradition of worship. Hannah, the mother of Samuel (who anointed Saul and David), stood when she prayed to the Lord for a son. (cf. 1 Sam. 1:26) Azariah, one of the three Jewish youths tossed into the furnace by King Nebuchadnezzar for refusing to worship the idols he created, stood in the midst of the fire to pray. (cf. Dan. 3:25) It was still a common posture for prayer in 1st century Israel as well; Jesus mentions it three times. (cf. Matt. 6:5; Mark 11:25; Luke 18:11-13) When St. Stephen, the first martyr, sees Jesus in Heaven at the right hand of the Father – where He is eternally interceding on our behalf – he sees Him standing. (cf. Acts 7:55; Rom. 8:34; Heb. 7:25)

For Catholics, praying while standing is jubilant prayer, "the posture of the victor," an "Easter form of prayer." (*The Spirit of the Liturgy*, p. 195) The first Council of Nicaea (A.D. 325) established a liturgical discipline that "On Sundays and during the Paschal season prayers should be said standing." (Canon 20) Standing is one side of reverence toward God. Standing is "the sign of vigilance and action" showing "the respect of the servant in attendance, of the soldier on duty." (*Sacred Signs*)

Standing is the default posture during Mass: from the beginning to the end of Mass we stand, except for the readings before the Gospel, the homily, the Offertory, the Eucharistic Prayer, after the "Lamb of God,"[2]

---

[2] The *General Instruction of the Roman Missal* allows the Bishop to change this posture: "The faithful kneel after the *Agnus Dei* unless the Diocesan Bishop determines otherwise." (GIRM 43)

and the moments after we have received Communion. We are standing at all other times. We are standing at attention in the house of God, waiting to hear His word and carry out His will.

Sitting

As commonplace as standing was for worship, we do know that there was *some* sitting in the liturgy of the early Church. St. Paul mentions people sitting near one another while prophesying (cf. 1 Cor. 14:30), and St. James cautions those who give seats of honor in the assembly to the rich while forcing the poor to stand or be humiliated. (cf. Jas. 2:2-4) Perhaps the most fitting example for us today is when Jesus visits the home of Martha and her sister Mary, "who sat at the Lord's feet and *listened to his teaching.*" (Luke 10:39) We don't sit during the Gospel, but we do sit as the deacon, priest, or bishop *teaches us* from the Scriptures and the whole Tradition of the Church during the homily.

Sitting is usually a posture that calls for meditation and *attentive* listening on the part of the one sitting. We sit during the readings before the Gospel, the homily, the Offertory, and the time after Communion. Sitting "should be at the service of recollection" so that "our hearing and understanding are unimpeded." (*The Spirit of the Liturgy*, p. 196)

Kneeling

In the post-modern – even post-Christian – world of today, kneeling is looked upon as a posture that is no longer necessary. Cardinal Ratzinger provides two modern hypothetical arguments against kneeling: "It's not right for a grown man to do this – he should face God on his feet," and "It's not appropriate for redeemed man – he has been set free by Christ and doesn't need to kneel any more." (*The Spirit of the Liturgy*, p. 185) On the contrary, Ratzinger shows that kneeling is a posture learned through knowledge of God, and the early Church gives strong witness to its use.

The Hebrew words for "knee" and "to kneel" sound similar: *berek* and *barak*. Because the knees were a symbol of strength to the Hebrews, "to bend the knee [is] to bend our strength before the living God." (*The Spirit of the Liturgy*, p. 191) Throughout Scripture, we read of people kneeling or falling to their knees. After the Temple in Jerusalem was completed, King Solomon knelt on a platform in the Temple in the sight of all who were assembled, and he prayed aloud in thanksgiving and supplication to the Lord. (cf. Chr. 6:13ff) After fasting, Ezra fell to his knees and prayed to God in sorrow and contrition for the sins of his people. (cf. Ezra 9:5ff) Psalm 95:6 identifies bowing and kneeling as expressions of worship before the majesty of God. The prophet Daniel prayed on his knees facing Jerusalem three times a day. (cf. Dan. 6:10)

In the gospels, people who come up to Jesus to ask for healing often fall to their knees in His presence, whether lepers (cf. Mark 1:40), parents of those possessed by demons (cf. Matt. 17:14), rulers (cf. Matt. 9:18), or Gentile women. (cf. Matt. 15:25) St. Peter "fell down at Jesus' knees" in contrition when he witnessed a miraculous catch of fish at the Lord's command. (Luke 5:8) The mother of two of Jesus' apostles kneeled before Him to ask a favor (cf. Matt. 20:20), as did a young man who sought His wisdom on attaining eternal life. (cf. Mark 10:17)

During His agony in the Garden of Gethsemane, St. Luke records that Jesus *himself* knelt to pray to His Father. (cf. Luke 22:14) Cardinal Ratzinger notes that St. Luke records the parallels between St. Stephen's martyrdom and the Passion and crucifixion of Christ (for Whom Stephen was dying): as Stephen is being stoned, he kneels and prays aloud, "Lord Jesus, receive my spirit" (Acts 7:59; cf. Luke 23:46) and "Lord, do not hold this sin against them." (Acts 7:60; cf. Luke 23:34) These similarites lead Cardinal Ratzinger to conclude that:

> Kneeling is not only a Christian gesture, but a *Christological* one. ...
> The expression used by St. Luke to describe the kneeling of Christians (*theis ta gonata*) is unknown in classical Greek. We are dealing here with a specifically Christian word. (*The Spirit of the Liturgy*, pp. 192-194)

Elsewhere in the book of Acts, we read that St. Peter (9:40), St. Paul (20:36), and indeed the whole Christian community (21:5) prayed on their knees. In his letter to the Ephesians, St. Paul confesses "I bow my knees before the Father." (Eph. 3:14) In the heavenly liturgy described in the book of the Revelation, St. John sees "the four living creatures and the twenty-four elders [falling] down before the Lamb" in worship. (Rev. 5:8) St. Paul interprets the words of God in Isaiah 45:23 – "to me every knee shall bow, every tongue shall swear" – in light of Jesus Christ: *"at the name of Jesus* every knee should bow ... and every tongue confess *that Jesus*

Christ is Lord." (Phil. 2:10-11) In a story from the Desert Fathers, the devil is characterized as *having no knees.* "The inability to kneel is seen as the very essence of the diabolical." (*The Spirit of the Liturgy,* p. 193)

Kneeling and standing are the two sides of reverence; kneeling is "the side of worship in rest and quietness." (*Sacred Signs*) In its various contexts, it conveys adoration, petition, and contrition. During the Mass, we kneel for the Eucharistic Prayer, after the "Lamb of God,"[3] and, if we so choose, after receiving Communion. We kneel at the death of the Lord during the reading of the Passion, and during the Prayer of the Faithful on Good Friday.

Bowing

There are two forms of bowing: a bow of the head and a bow of the body (bending at the waist, known as a "profound bow"). Bowing, like kneeling, is a way of expressing humility and honor. In Luke 18:9-14, Jesus tells the parable of the Pharisee and the tax collector who go to the temple to pray; both stand to pray, but the tax collector *"would not even lift up his eyes* to heaven, but beat his breast, saying, 'God, be merciful to me a sinner!'" The word *supplices* is found in the first sentence of the Roman Canon (Eucharistic Prayer I); this Latin word denotes beseeching or imploring God in humility ("supplication"). Cardinal Ratzinger translates the word as *"bowing low, we implore thee."* (*The Spirit of the Liturgy,* p. 205)

Throughout the liturgy, a bow of the head is made whenever the three Divine Persons are named together ("the Father, the Son, and the Holy Spirit"), as well as at the name of Jesus. This was codified by Pope Gregory X at the Second Council of Lyons in 1274:

> Each should fulfill in himself that which is written for all that *at the name of Jesus* every knee should bow; whenever that glorious name is recalled, especially during the sacred mysteries of the Mass, *everyone should bow the knees of his heart,* which he can do even *by a bow of his head.* (Constitution 25)

A bow of the head is also made at Mary's name and at the name of the saint(s) being honored that day. If you receive Holy Communion standing, you should make a bow of the head as a sign of reverence just before you receive. (cf. GIRM 275a, 160)

---

[3] For differences in posture after the "Lamb of God," see page 36, footnote 2.

A bow of the body is made to the altar (which is a symbol of Christ) and also during the Profession of Faith – during the words "by the Holy Spirit was incarnate of the Virgin Mary, and became man" in the Nicene Creed, and the words "who was conceived by the Holy Spirit, born of the Virgin Mary" in the Apostles' Creed. (cf. GIRM 275b) This bow in the Creed is replaced by a genuflection on two solemnities, explained below.

Genuflecting

A few times in the liturgy, we are called to make a genuflection. This posture is sometimes confused with kneeling, since the word "genuflect" comes from the two Latin words *genu* and *flecto* which literally mean "to bend the knee." To genuflect is to lower *one* knee to the ground while keeping your head and back straight. It is not a curtsey.

This posture is reserved for the Blessed Sacrament (whether in the tabernacle or exposed in a monstrance) and, on Good Friday, for the crucifix during its veneration. On the solemnities of the Annunciation of our Lord (March 25) and the Nativity of our Lord (December 25), we genuflect (instead of bow) during the words "by the Holy Spirit was incarnate of the Virgin Mary, and became man" in the Nicene Creed, and the words "who was conceived by the Holy Spirit, born of the Virgin Mary" in the Apostles' Creed. (cf. GIRM 137) It is customary to show reverence to the Blessed Sacrament reserved in the tabernacle by genuflecting towards the tabernacle[4] when entering or exiting a pew (or a church), although this is done *before* and *after* Mass, not *during* Mass. You should also genuflect if you pass in front of the Blessed Sacrament, unless you are part of a procession, in which case you should bow your head. (cf. GIRM 274) If you are unable to genuflect due to age or injury, a bow (either of the head or of the body) is permissible.

There is an inseparable bond between our posture and gestures and our spiritual disposition:

---

[4] If there is a lamp or candle burning near the tabernacle, that means the Blessed Sacrament is present. There is no need to genuflect to an *empty* tabernacle, because it is not the tabernacle you reverence but Who is *inside* it, Jesus Christ present in the Eucharist.

> Without the worship, the bodily gesture would be meaningless, while the spiritual act must of its very nature ... express itself in the bodily gesture. ... When someone tries to take worship back into the purely spiritual realm and refuses to give it embodied form, the act of worship evaporates, for what is purely spiritual is inappropriate to the nature of man. (*The Spirit of the Liturgy*, p. 191)

The Catholic Church has an "Incarnational" worship: because the Lord came in human flesh, our worship of God is not just done in spirit, but "in spirit and truth" (John 4:24), and that truth includes the reality of our physical bodies. (cf. *Catechism* 1146) John Henry Cardinal Newman, a 19th century Anglican convert, said that because the One Who created us gave us both body and soul,

> Our tongues must preach Him, and our voices sing of Him, and our knees adore Him, and our hands supplicate Him, and our heads bow before Him, and our countenances beam of Him, and our gait herald Him. ("The Visible Temple", *Parochial and Plain Sermons*, p. 1365)

Questions for Reflection

1) **Interpret:** God promised to the Patriarchs (Abraham, Isaac, and Jacob) that He would be with them (cf. Gen. 17:21; 26:24; 28:15). Why is God's presence and assistance so important in our lives, and especially in the Mass?

2) **Interpret:** In the Old Testament, how did God's faithful (such as Moses and Elijah) react when He manifested Himself to them?

3) **Explain:** Why do we stand for the Gospel but not for the other readings?

4) **Explain:** How can bodily gestures be prayers? How can they be acts of worship?

5) **Explain:** Almost every prayer said during the Mass is said while the person praying it is standing. What significance does posture give to prayer?

6) **Relate:** What are you saying *Amen* to when you receive Holy Communion?

7) **Relate:** Our Lord tells us that He is present to us in the least of our brethren. (cf. Matt. 25:31-46) How should the reverence we show to the Lord in the Mass shape our respect for one another, especially those who are denied their dignity by the world?

"Hear, O Lord, and have mercy,
for we have sinned before you."
(Baruch 3:2)

"But the tax collector, standing far off, would not even lift up his eyes to
heaven, but beat his breast, saying, 'God, be merciful to me a sinner!'"
(Luke 18:13)

4

Penitential Act

WHEN JESUS ENTERED Jerusalem during the week of His Crucifixion (on the day we commemorate as Palm Sunday), He went into the Temple area and "caused a scene." He drove out the money-changers, men who "helped" Jews on pilgrimage by trading their foreign currency for the coinage used in the Temple... at a lousy exchange rate. After chastising these dishonest bankers, Jesus turned His attention to the blind and the lame, whom He healed. We commemorate – and enter into – His cleansing of the Temple and His healing of the infirm at every Mass. It is called the Penitential Act.

The purpose of the Penitential Act, in the words of the Missal itself, is to "prepare ourselves to celebrate the sacred mysteries." To do this in honesty and sincerity before God, we must examine ourselves and admit our sin and our sinfulness, asking the Lord for His mercy. Jesus tells us to be reconciled with one another before we present our offerings and ourselves at the altar. (cf. Matt. 5:23-24) In the words of the Catechism, "the first movement of the prayer of petition is *asking forgiveness*. ... It is a prerequisite for righteous and pure prayer." (*Catechism* 2631) This is true both in the liturgy and in our personal prayer.

After the priest invites us into this act, there is a brief pause for silent reflection and examination. Make proper use of this silence by calling to mind your sins – the ways you have failed to live out the Gospel in your daily life – and repenting of them. There has been a loss of the sense of sin in our world, with dangerous effects: so long as we're healthy, wealthy, and wise (in the eyes of the world) we think we're "all right." On the contrary, Rev. Thomas Kocik wrote in *Loving and Living the Mass* that Jesus might say in our contemporary language, "it is better to enter heaven with a guilt complex than to enter Gehenna brimming with self-confidence." (p. 43)

So how is this anything similar to the wild-but-tender side of Christ that we see in Matthew 21:12-14? "Do you not know that your body is a temple of the Holy Spirit within you?" (1 Cor. 6:19) "We are the temple of the living God." (2 Cor. 6:16) We are temples, but we are marred by the stain of sin, as guilty as the money-changers though our sins might be completely different. We are temples, but we are plagued with sickness, as in need of Christ's healing touch as were the blind and the lame. In the Penitential Act, Jesus Christ comes to us to cleanse us and to heal us of our sins.[1]

There are three forms that the Penitential Act can take.

Form A, "I confess…"

Form A, known as the *Confiteor* (the first word of the prayer in Latin), is a penitential prayer in two parts. The first part of this prayer is an act of confession of personal sin to God, in the midst of the whole assembly.

Confíteor Deo omnipoténti et vobis, fratres,
quia peccávi nimis cogitatióne, verbo, ópere et omissióne:

I confess to almighty God	*Ps. 51:5-6; Luke 15:18; 1 John 1:9*
and to you, my brothers and sisters,	*Jas. 5:16*
» that I have greatly sinned	*2 Sam. 24:10*
in my thoughts and in my words,	*Wis. 1:3; Jas. 3:8-10*
in what I have done and in what I have failed to do,	*Rom. 7:15-20; Jas. 2:17*

---

[1] The Penitential Act in the Mass *does not* replace the sacramental confession of sins, and mortal sins especially can only ordinarily be absolved through the sacrament of Reconciliation.

Although it is said by all the congregation together, it is a *personal* prayer. The *Confiteor* is one of only three places[2] in the Mass where we pray in the first-personal singular (I) rather than the first-person plural (we). We confess our sins not only to God but to all those present. Talk about accountability! Even though we are not *naming* our sins to those around us, we are admitting our guilt to them. The *Confiteor* is inspired by David's sorrowful plea for mercy in Psalm 51.

We confess that our sins are of thought and word, of omission and commission. Jesus never had an evil thought, never spoke an evil word (not even when He was chastising the Pharisees for their blindness), never did anything wrong, and never *failed* to do the *right thing*. It's a tough act to follow, but with the grace of God – which comes to us especially through frequent sacramental Confession and reception of Holy Communion – we can be built up "to the measure of the stature of the fullness of Christ." (Eph. 4:13)

The first half of the *Confiteor* ends with an admission of *personal* guilt for our sins. As we say these words, we strike our breast three times in a sign of penitence:

mea culpa, mea culpa, mea máxima culpa.

» through my fault, through my fault,   *Sir. 20:2b*
» through my most grievous fault;

The repetition of this admission of guilt adds to its severity. We do not say "The devil made me do it, the devil made me do it, you can *bet* the devil made me do it," but accuse only ourselves for our sins. We beat our breast with a closed fist, like the tax collector who prayed from his heart, "God, be merciful to me a sinner!" (Luke 18:13) Concerning the gravity of these words and this gesture, Cardinal Ratzinger wrote:

> We point not at someone else but at ourselves as the guilty party, [which] remains a meaningful gesture of prayer. ... When we say *mea culpa* (through my fault), we turn, so to speak, to ourselves, to our own front door, and thus we are able rightly to ask forgiveness of God, the saints, and the people gathered around us, whom we have wronged. (*The Spirit of the Liturgy*, p. 207)

---

[2] The second is in the Creed ("*I* believe…", chapter 7), but it is used for a different reason there. The third is the "Lord, *I* am not worthy…" (chapter 11)

Rev. Romano Guardini explained that the meaning of this gesture of contrition depends upon it being done properly:

> To brush one's clothes with the tips of one's fingers is not to strike the breast. We should beat upon our breasts with our closed fists. ... It is an honest blow, not an elegant gesture. To strike the breast is to beat against the gates of our inner world in order to shatter them. This is its significance. ... "Repent, do penance." It is the voice of God. Striking the breast is the visible sign that we hear that summons. ... Let it wake us up, and make us see, and turn to God. (*Sacred Signs*)

The *Douay Catechism* (from 1649), a question-and-answer catechism on the doctrines of the Church, included a chapter expounding the essence and ceremonies of the Mass. It explains that the reason for striking the heart is "to teach the people to return into the heart" because it "signifies that all sin is from the heart, and ought to be discharged from the heart, with hearty sorrow." (p. 125)

In the second half of the prayer, we invoke the communion of saints as we ask for the prayers of the whole Church:

Ideo precor beátam Maríam semper Vírginem, omnes Angelos et Sanctos, et vos, fratres, oráre pro me ad Dóminum Deum nostrum.

» therefore I ask blessed Mary ever-Virgin,[3]   *John 19:26-27; Jas. 5:16*
all the Angels and Saints,   *Heb. 12:1,22-24; Rev. 5:8; 8:3-4*
and you, my brothers and sisters,   *1 Th. 5:25; 1 John 5:16*
to pray for me to the Lord our God.   *1 Sam. 12:23; Bar. 1:13*

In Hebrews 11, we are given a tour of God's Hall of Fame, a list of men and women who, by their faith in God, "received divine approval." The list includes Abel, Noah, Abram, Sarah, Joseph, Moses, and Rahab. At the end of the list, we read:

> Therefore, since *we are surrounded by so great a cloud of witnesses*, let us also lay aside every weight, and sin which clings so closely, and let us run with perseverance the race that is set before us, looking to Jesus the pioneer and perfecter of our faith, who for the joy that was set before him endured the cross, despising the shame, and is seated at the right hand of the throne of God. (Heb. 12:1-2)

We learn something very encouraging from this passage: the saints in Heaven are *witnesses* to our lives on earth, witnesses who cheer us on

---

[3] The *Confiteor* expresses the faith of the Church in the *perpetual virginity* of Mary.

and pray for us, that we might endure the trials of this life and join the saints in Heaven having won "the crown of life which God has promised to those who love him." (Jas. 1:12) The prayers of the saints and angels in Heaven are of great worth to us, because the saints have been perfected and have "washed their robes and made them white in the blood of the Lamb" (Rev. 7:14) and the angels rejoice greatly when a sinner repents. (cf. Luke 15:7) See chapter 7 ("Profession of Faith") for more about the communion of saints.

But we don't only ask the Church Triumphant (in Heaven) for their prayers, we also ask *one another* for prayers. The next time you say these words at Mass, take a moment to look at the people around you: you are asking these people, sinners though they are, to pray to God for you, a sinner.

Form B

In the second form, the priest and the congregation speak two prayers for mercy from Scripture. First, the priest says "Have mercy on us, O Lord," to which we respond:

Quia peccávimus tibi.

» For we have sinned against you.   *Bar. 3:2*

The priest speaks the first half of Baruch 3:2, and we respond with the second half.[4] This profession of guilt reminds us of our need to live holy lives "worthy of the calling to which [we] have been called." (Eph. 4:1) The plea for mercy reminds us of how ready God is to bestow the abundance of His gracious mercy upon us.

The new translation is a vast improvement over the old one, which completely re-arranged this first half of the prayer (switching the words of the priest with the words of the congregation) and duplicated the phrase "Lord, have mercy." The duplication of that phrase may have led some people to think that Form B of the Penitential Act included the *Kyrie* (which it does not), thereby omitting the *Kyrie* from the Mass altogether!

---

[4] This verse from Baruch is the antiphon of the Lenten hymn *Attende Domine* ("Hear us, O Lord").

Then the priest says "Show us, O Lord, your mercy," to which we respond:

Et salutáre tuum da nobis.

And grant us your salvation. *Ps. 85:7*

Again, the priest begins a verse from the Psalms and we complete it. We do not simply ask the Lord for mercy, but for His salvation. The Lord Jesus did not come to earth simply to forgive our sins, but to "lead us, with our sins forgiven, to *eternal life*," as the priest says in the prayer at the end of the Penitential Act. Through Jesus Christ, we have not only the forgiveness of our sins, but the hope of eternal salvation.

Form C

The third form of the Penitential Act integrates three invocations to the Lord Jesus Christ with the *Kyrie*. The invocations by the priest, deacon, or cantor can vary (and the Missal provides particular formulas), but the responses are always the same and are covered next.

"Lord, have mercy."

If Form A or Form B of the Penitential Act is used, it is followed by the *Kyrie*.[5] The acclamations "*Kyrie, eleison*" and "*Christe, eleison*" are Greek for "Lord, have mercy" and "Christ, have mercy." Even when the Mass is celebrated entirely in Latin, this part of the Mass is never translated from Greek to Latin, in homage to the Greek heritage of Christianity.

Kýrie, eléison.
Christe, eléison.
Kýrie, eléison.

Lord, have mercy. *Ps. 123:3; Matt. 20:31; Luke 17:13*
Christ, have mercy. *1 Tim. 1:2; Jude 1:21*
Lord, have mercy.

These acclamations are said two or three times. The repetition is a sign of their urgency and fervency: we are always in need of God's mercy, and there is never a reason to delay seeking it.

---

[5] The *Kyrie* is omitted when Form C is used.

We are not only praying for mercy for *ourselves*. Because we are baptized into the Body of Christ, we share in His priesthood. Part of our baptismal priesthood is offering prayers and interceding on behalf of others, especially those who cannot (or *do* not) pray for themselves.

Sprinkling with Holy Water

On Sundays, especially during the Easter season, the Penitential Act can be replaced by the sprinkling of the congregation with holy water as a reminder of our Baptism. As this is being done, an appropriate chant is sung which calls to mind the purifying power which God has given to the waters of Baptism. The traditional chant used during the Easter season is the *Vidi aquam* (cf. Ezek. 47:1-2); outside of the Easter Season, the chant *Asperges Me* (cf. Psalm 51:7) is used. Yet another chant comes from the words of God proclaimed through the prophet Ezekiel:

> "*I will sprinkle clean water upon you*, and you shall be clean from all your uncleannesses, and from all your idols I will cleanse you. A new heart I will give you, and *a new spirit I will put within you*; and I will take out of your flesh the heart of stone and give you a heart of flesh." (Ezek. 36:25-26)

When we are sprinkled with the holy water, we make the Sign of the Cross again. The Cross and water are two signs explicitly connected to one another by Jesus Christ at His Crucifixion: after He had breathed His last, a soldier pierced His side with a lance, and water and blood flowed forth from His side. (cf. John 19:34; 1 John 5:6) Just as Eve was fashioned from the side of Adam as he slept (cf. Gen. 2:21-22), so too the Church was born out of the side of Christ as He hung in the sleep of death on the Cross. The "living water" (John 4:10) which came from the side of Christ is a sign of Baptism, as the blood is a sign of the Eucharist.

We know that we are unworthy before God and that we cannot earn the gift of salvation; it is only through His grace that we are saved. However, once we have been brought into this new life of grace and mercy, we are compelled to change our ways and to live in a way that glorifies Jesus for His great sacrifice for us.

I liken it to a young boy who receives a gift from his father one day, the father's favorite suit jacket. Of course, it doesn't fit the boy: his arms are too short, his shoulders aren't broad enough, and the jacket reaches the ground when he tries it on. The boy didn't do anything to deserve or earn this jacket, but the father was moved with love for the boy to give it to him anyway. The jacket is a sort of "goal" for the boy, something to strive for. Over the years, if he keeps himself healthy and avoids abusing his body, he will finally fit into that jacket his father gave him: he will *grow into* the gift he was given, it will not have been given to him in vain, he will have become worthy of it.

St. Paul made it clear to the churches he wrote to that they, like that young boy, must live worthily of the gift they had received, lest they end up receiving it in vain:

> Working together with him, then, we entreat you *not to accept the grace of God in vain.* (2 Cor. 6:1)

> I ... beg you to *lead a life worthy of the calling* to which you have been called, with all lowliness and meekness, with patience, forbearing one another in love, eager to maintain the unity of the Spirit in the bond of peace. (Eph. 4:1-3)

> Only *let your manner of life be worthy of the gospel of Christ,* ... stand[ing] firm in one spirit, with one mind striving side by side for the faith of the gospel. (Phil. 1:27)

> *Be blameless and innocent,* children of God without blemish in the midst of a crooked and perverse generation, among whom you shine as lights in the world, holding fast the word of life, so that in the day of Christ *I may be proud that I did not run in vain or labor in vain.* (Phil. 2:15-16)

> We have not ceased to pray for you, asking that you may be filled with the knowledge of his will in all spiritual wisdom and understanding, *to lead a life worthy of the Lord,* fully pleasing to him, bearing fruit in every good work and increasing in the knowledge of God. (Col. 1:9-10)

> We exhorted each one of you ... to *walk in a manner worthy of God,* who calls you into his own kingdom and glory. (1 Th. 2:11-12)

The Penitential Act is the first of many moments at Mass when we recall that we are sinners who need the grace of God in order to live worthily of the Gospel of Christ. We know we are not blameless and innocent, but we desperately desire to walk in a manner worthy of God, and so we must repent and implore the Lord's mercy. Try making an examination of conscience on your way to Mass so that you can be better prepared for the Penitential Act.

Our spiritual worship of God requires our temples be cleared of all profane influences. Having sought the Lord's forgiveness, we can enter into the prayer of the Mass as one whole body, the Church.

Questions for Reflection

1) **Interpret:** In his ministry, John the Baptist cried out "Repent, for the kingdom of heaven is at hand!" (Matt. 3:2) Jesus took up this same cry and added these important words: "Believe in the gospel." (Mark 1:15) Why is repentance necessary as a first step to accepting the Gospel of Jesus Christ?

2) **Interpret:** In the parable of the Prodigal Son (cf. Luke 15:11-32), Jesus describes the lengths to which God goes to reconcile us to Himself again. Meditate on verse 20: "He arose and came to his father. But *while he was yet at a distance, his father saw him* and had compassion, and ran and embraced him and kissed him." How does this parable change the way you look at the Penitential Act?

3) **Explain:** What does the gesture of striking the breast mean to you?

4) **Explain:** Read Psalm 51. What symbolism do you seen in being sprinkled with holy water?

5) **Relate:** In the *Confiteor*, we ask our brothers and sisters to pray for us. When is the last time *you* prayed for *them*?

6) **Relate:** How is God's mercy related to the mission He entrusted to the Church to spread the Gospel throughout the whole world? How does receiving God's mercy help *you* fulfill this mission?

"Bless the Lord, you angels of the Lord,
sing praise to him and highly exalt him for ever."
(Daniel 3:37)

Suddenly there was with the angel
a multitude of the heavenly host praising God.
(Luke 2:13)

5

The *Gloria*

THE MASS IS AN encounter with the mystery of God through the unfolding of His plan of redemption for us. We began with the Sign of the Cross, the sign of our salvation; then we implored Christ, Who shed His blood on the Cross so that sins might be forgiven, to have mercy on us and forgive us our sins. Now we commemorate that singular and most wondrous mystery by which our redemption was actually made possible: the Incarnation. God Almighty, Creator of all that exists, condescended to come among us in our human flesh, and humbled Himself to be born of a woman, to suffer and die for us on a cross, to reconcile us back to Himself. For this, we give God glory.

The *Gloria* is a joyful response to the forgiveness received in the Penitential Act. When it was first introduced to the Roman liturgy, it was sung only at the midnight celebration of the Nativity of our Lord. It is called the "Angelic Hymn" because it begins with the song of the angels which was heard at the birth of Jesus Christ. (cf. Luke 2:13-14) It is also called the "Major Doxology" because it is great prayer of glory to God: the word *doxology* comes from the Greek *doxa* ("glory", *gloria* in Latin) and *logos* ("word, speaking"), literally meaning "word(s) of glory."

Glória in excélsis Deo et in terra pax homínibus bonæ voluntátis.

Glory to God in the highest,   *Luke 2:14*
» and on earth peace to people of good will.

This is the first of two places in the Mass where we take upon our lips the words of the angels: these words were sung by the angels on earth at the nativity of our Lord, when the Incarnation was made manifest to the lowly shepherds of Bethlehem. It is a reminder that, in the Mass, Heaven and earth are mystically joined; as it was explained at Vatican II:

> In the earthly liturgy we take part in *a foretaste of that heavenly liturgy* which is celebrated in the holy city of Jerusalem toward which we journey as pilgrims, where Christ is sitting at the right hand of God, a minister of the holies and of the true tabernacle; *we sing a hymn to the Lord's glory with all the warriors of the heavenly army;* venerating the memory of the saints, we hope for some part and fellowship with them; we eagerly await the Savior, Our Lord Jesus Christ, until He, our life, shall appear and we too will appear with Him in glory. (CSL 8)

In the Penitential Act, we asked to be forgiven of our sins. Now the angels announce "peace to people of good will," which is one of the characteristics of the eternal covenant established through Jesus Christ:

> "*My servant David shall be king* over them; and they shall all have *one shepherd.* ... I will make *a covenant of peace* with them; it shall be an everlasting covenant with them; and I will bless them and multiply them, and will set *my sanctuary in the midst of them* for evermore. *My dwelling place shall be with them;* and I will be their God, and they shall be my people." (Ezek. 37:24-27)

In Ezekiel 34, God laments the false shepherds who have not been guarding Israel. First, He announces that He Himself shall be Israel's shepherd (cf. Ezek. 34:15); then He says: "I will set up over them one shepherd, my servant David." (Ezek. 34:23; cf. 37:24) This duality of God *and* His servant "David"[1] being the *one* shepherd of His people mystically foreshadows the Incarnation of the Son of God, to Whom God the Father will give "the throne of his father David." (Luke 1:32)

The *Gloria* continues with praise of God the Father for His majesty:

---

[1] This prophecy of Ezekiel was received during the time when Israel was split in two, long after King David had died, so when David is mentioned it is a reference to a Davidic king.

Laudámus te, benedícimus te, adorámus te, glorificámus te,
grátias ágimus tibi propter magnam glóriam tuam,
Dómine Deus, Rex cæléstis, Deus Pater omnípotens.

» We praise you, we bless you,	*Bar. 3:6; Ps. 145:2*
» we adore you, we glorify you,	*Rev. 4:11; Rom. 11:36; 1 Cor. 6:20*
» we give you thanks for your great glory,	*1 Chr. 16:24; 2 Cor. 4:15*
» Lord God, heavenly King,	*Rev. 4:8; Tob. 13:7; Dan. 4:37*
» O God, almighty Father.	*Gen. 17:1; 2 Cor. 6:18*

Here we carry out two of the four ends of prayer, which are *adoration* and *thanksgiving*. We praise, bless, adore, glorify, and thank God for the glory He has revealed to us. While the old text summarized all these verbs – "we worship you, we give you thanks, we praise you for your glory" – the new text translates each one individually. It might seem a little repetitive, but those words don't all have the *exact* same meaning. The abundance of words is a reminder of how constant our praise of God should be. It is also a sign of our inability to describe our response to God's greatness with just one or two words. Instead of just *praising* God for His glory (as in the old translation), we *thank* Him for His *great glory*: we're thanking God for *being God*.

The next part focuses on God the Son, Jesus Christ: the Father and the Son are both invoked as *Domine Deus*, "Lord God," affirming the equality of the Father and the Son. After invoking Jesus by several of His titles, we pray a three-fold litany asking Him to have mercy on us and hear our prayers:

Dómine Fili Unigénite, Iesu Christe,
Dómine Deus, Agnus Dei, Fílius Patris,
qui tollis peccáta mundi, miserére nobis;
qui tollis peccáta mundi, súscipe deprecatiónem nostram.
Qui sedes ad déxteram Patris, miserére nobis.

» Lord Jesus Christ, Only Begotten Son,	*John 1:14,18*
» Lord God, Lamb of God, Son of the Father,	*Rev. 1:8; John 1:29*
you take away the sins of the world, have mercy on us;	*John 1:29*
» you take away the sins of the world, receive our prayer;	*John 14:13*
you are seated at the right hand of the Father,	*Col. 3:1; Heb. 8:1*
» have mercy on us.	

There is an axiom of the Church which states that "the law of prayer is the law of belief" (*lex orandi, lex credendi*); in other words, *how* we pray reflects and shapes *what* we believe. Through the many titles for Jesus that are we invoke, the *Gloria* describes our faith in *Who* Jesus *is.* This displays the catechetical power of the prayers of the Mass. What these titles mean will be explained in greater detail in later chapters.

The three-fold litany (which was reduced to only two in the old translation) provides the other two ends of prayer: *contrition* and *petition.* We again ask the Lord for mercy (twice) and we beseech Him to hear us when we pray. These four ends of prayer – adoration, thanksgiving, contrition, and petition – are summed up here in the hymn we sing most Sundays of the year. The *Gloria,* along with the Our Father, should be a model for personal prayer as well: glorify God and give Him thanks first, *then* present your needs to Him.

The hymn ends with a brief Trinitarian doxology. We profess the Son, the Spirit, and the Father as the one Holy and Most High Lord:

**Quóniam tu solus Sanctus, tu solus Dóminus,
tu solus Altíssimus, Iesu Christe,
cum Sancto Spíritu: in glória Dei Patris. Amen.**

For you alone are the Holy One,	*Rev. 15:4*
you alone are the Lord,	*Isa. 37:20*
you alone are the Most High, Jesus Christ,	*Ps. 83:18*
with the Holy Spirit,	*Rom 8:9; 1 Pet. 3:8*
in the glory of God the Father. Amen.	*Luke 9:26; John 1:14; Phil. 2:11*

The word "alone" here (*solus* in the Latin, *monos* in the Greek) might be misleading. It does not mean that Jesus is *alone,* for God is a living communion of three Persons, and neither the Father, nor the Son, nor the Holy Spirit can be "alone." Rather, it means "only," in the sense that there is only One Who is Holy, the Lord, the Most High, and that One is three Persons. The affirmation that Jesus Christ is the Most High is another clear identification of Jesus with God.

Ordinarily, the *Gloria* is sung or recited on Sundays, solemnities, and feast days; it is omitted on other weekdays. However, it is also omitted during two liturgical seasons of the Church: Advent and Lent (except when a solemnity, like the Immaculate Conception or the Annunciation, occurs during that season). During Advent, the *Gloria* is omitted in anticipation of its first singing by the angels at Bethlehem. During Lent, it is omitted because of the somber and penitential nature of the season; we consider what our lives would be like if Christ had not come to save us. It is sung with great joy and fervor at the Mass of the Lord's Supper on Holy Thursday, with bells ringing… and then those bells are silent again until the Easter Vigil.

After the *Gloria*, the priest calls us to prayer: "*Oremus*. Let us pray." Before he prays the Collect (so named because it *collects* the intentions and prayers of the Mass into one), there is a moment of silence. Why? So that *we can pray*. This silence is not an awkward pause while the priest leafs through the Missal to find the right prayer, it is a time of silence for us to *collect* our own thoughts and prayers, and to prepare to unite them to the Collect which will set the tone for the rest of the Mass. When he has finished the Collect, we give our assent by saying "Amen" – so make sure you've listened to what it is we're praying for! He makes this prayer through Christ our Lord, Whom we have just entreated in the *Gloria* to "receive our prayer." Jesus Christ hears us, we can be sure, because He answers us with the greatest answer to prayer: Himself, the Living and Eternal Word of God, in the Liturgy of the Word.

Questions for Reflection

1) **Interpret:** Why does the *Gloria* begin with the words sung by the angels at the birth of Christ? How is the Incarnation linked to the rest of God's great works? How does it bring about peace for "people of good will"?

2) **Explain:** Read Revelation 4-5. During the *Gloria*, we make a bow of the head at both invocations of the name of Jesus; how does this reflect the reverence shown by the angels and elders in Heaven to Jesus, the Lamb?

3) **Relate:** How can you make your private prayer more like the *Gloria*?

4) **Relate:** What does the Incarnation mean for you as a Catholic? What significance does the Incarnation have for each and every human person?

Joshua said to the sons of Israel,
"Come here, and hear the words of the LORD your God."
(Joshua 3:9)

Blessed is he who reads aloud the words of the prophecy,
and blessed are those who hear, and who keep what is written therein.
(Revelation 1:3)

6

Liturgy of the Word

THERE WAS A pastor in a small parish known for his monotone voice and his long, rambling homilies. At weekday Masses, he would do all the readings himself. One morning, as he was droning through the First Reading, he began to lose his voice. It became fainter and weaker until he reached the end of the reading. He tried to say "The word of the Lord," but he couldn't make a sound. He tried again, but still nothing came out. He leaned as close to the microphone as he could and managed to groan "I think I've lost my voice." The congregation responded, "Thanks be to God."

"Thanks be to God."

When the reader or Lector finishes the First (or Second) Reading and says "The word of the Lord," we respond:

Deo grátias.

Thanks be to God. *Rom. 7:25; 2 Cor. 9:15*

The story above was funny, sure, but it begs the question: *what* are we thanking God for when we say "Thanks be to God"? The two passages referred to, from Romans 7 and 2 Corinthians 9, give us some insight.

In Romans 7, St. Paul writes about the internal struggle we all face, even after Baptism: we do the evil which we do not want to do, and we do not do the good which we want to do:

> I do not understand my own actions. *For I do not do what I want, but I do the very thing I hate.* ... I can *will* what is right, but I cannot *do* it. For I do not do the good I want, but the evil I do not want is what I do. ... So I find it to be a law that when I want to do right, evil lies close at hand. For I delight in the law of God, in my inmost self, but I see in my members another law at war with the law of my mind and making me captive to the law of sin which dwells in my members. Wretched man that I am! Who will deliver me from this body of death? *Thanks be to God through Jesus Christ our Lord!* So then, I of myself serve the law of God with my mind, but with my flesh I serve the law of sin. (Rom. 7:15-25)

This conflict between his "inmost self" (his soul which has received an indelible mark in Baptism) and his "members" (his flesh which is still under the power of his earthly desires) is common to all of us: the term the Church uses for it is *concupiscence*, the tendency of human nature to sin as a result of our inability to subordinate our desires to the dictates of reason. Faced with his own wretchedness, St. Paul thanks God for His Son Jesus Christ Who delivers him from his "body of death."

In 2 Corinthians 9, St. Paul is writing about the generosity of the people of Corinth. The Corinthians were such zealous and ready givers that he had bragged about them to others in Macedonia. He tells them that their generosity is only possible because of God's generosity: "God is able to provide you with every blessing in abundance, so that you may always have enough of everything and may provide in abundance for every good work." (2 Cor. 9:8) He concludes:

> You will be enriched in every way for great generosity, which through us will produce *thanksgiving to God*; for the rendering of this service not only supplies the wants of the saints but also overflows in *many thanksgivings to God.* Under the test of this service, you will glorify God by your obedience in acknowledging the gospel of Christ, and by the generosity of your contribution for them and for all others; while they long for you and pray for you, because of *the surpassing grace of God in you. Thanks be to God for his inexpressible gift!* (2 Cor. 9:11-15)

Three times he speaks of thanks to God: thanksgiving for His great generosity of *grace*, the "inexpressible gift" of God.

It is for these two things that we say "Thanks be to God" at the end of the readings from Scripture. First and foremost, we recognize that in the Scriptures being proclaimed, we are hearing God's word which the Holy Spirit inspired various men to put into writing. In Scripture, the phrase "the word of the Lord" means, quite simply, a revelation directly from God. In Jesus, this Word of God is enfleshed: Christ is the Word-made-Flesh. As Vatican II said in the Dogmatic Constitution on Divine Revelation, *Dei Verbum* (DV), Jesus Christ "is both the mediator and the fullness of all revelation." (DV 2)

Secondly, we acknowledge the pure love that God shows for us in bestowing His "surpassing grace" upon us, that we may hear His word proclaimed to our ears. Jesus said "blessed are your eyes, for they see, and your ears, for they hear" (Matt. 13:16), and again, "Blessed rather are those who hear the word of God and keep it!" (Luke 11:28) St. John begins his book of Revelation with these words: "Blessed is he who reads aloud the words of the prophecy, and blessed are those who hear, and who keep what is written therein." (Rev. 1:3) There are many eyes and ears in the world that go without reading or hearing the Sacred Scriptures; as we thank God for His grace, we must not forget the mission of the Church to spread the Gospel throughout all the world.

Such a small phrase – "Thanks be to God!" – is an important and powerful prayer which you can offer in many situations throughout your day. We often fall into the trap of thinking that prayer has to be a long, drawn-out, distinctly liturgical process: kneeling beside your bed for ten minutes before bed, saying an Our Father, a Hail Mary, this prayer, that prayer, etc. While liturgical and ordered prayer is a wonderful thing, do not let the unpredictability of your day prevent you from offering up little "darts" of prayer to Heaven: "Jesus, I trust in you!" "Jesus, thank you for your mercy and your love!" "Thanks be to God!"

Responsorial Psalm or Gradual

Following the First Reading is a psalm, either the Responsorial Psalm or the Gradual. The Responsorial Psalm is generally thematically related to the First Reading and involves the vocal participation of the whole congregation in singing or saying at least the response (said in between the other verses), whereas the Gradual is more of a meditative piece of its own requiring vocal participation from the choir and conscious and attentive listening from the rest of the congregation.

The whole Mass is a prayer, but the Psalm in particular is a time when we all pray the very words of Scripture together. The book of Psalms (also called the *Psalter*) is the "hymnal" of the people of Israel:

> The Psalter consists of 150 psalms or sacred hymns. In it we find poetical compositions of different kinds – hymns of praise, prayers for specific liturgical occasions, lamentations both of the individual and the nation, among others. There are psalms that express the deepest emotions of the human heart. They were used in, and many of them composed for, the temple worship. Some of them date back to King David, others were written shortly after the Exile. Their composition thus covers a long period. They were gradually brought together in small collections finally edited in one large collection arranged in five books. This became the hymnbook of the Second Temple.
>
> The Christian Church took over the Psalter and used it following the example of Jesus himself. The Psalms have always been used extensively in the liturgy and in the daily office of the priest. In the early Church lay people became familiar with them, as St. Jerome tells us. (*Revised Standard Version Bible, 2nd Catholic Edition*, Ignatius Edition, p. 421)

Although the earliest Christians composed new hymns and songs to Christ (cf. 1 Cor. 14:26; Eph. 5:19; Col. 3:16), they never lost sight of the music of their Jewish heritage, the Psalms. The Christological nature of the Psalms was revealed over time, as shown by the number of references to the Psalms by the authors of the New Testament. St. Peter affirmed that Psalm 2 (specifically verse 7) and Psalm 16 (specifically verse 10) referred to Jesus:

> "And we bring you the good news that what God promised to the fathers this he has fulfilled to us their children by raising Jesus; as also it is written in the second psalm, 'You are my Son, today I have begotten you.' And as for the fact that he raised him from the dead, no more to return to corruption, he spoke in this way, 'I will give you the holy and sure blessings of David.' Therefore he says also in another psalm, 'You will not let your Holy One see corruption.' For David, after he had served the counsel of God in his own generation, fell asleep, and was laid with his fathers, and saw corruption; but he whom God raised up saw no corruption." (Acts 13:32-37)

After His Resurrection, Jesus told His disciples "that everything written about me in the law of Moses and the prophets and the psalms must be fulfilled." (Luke 24:44)

Gospel Acclamation

Just before the Gospel – the high point of the Liturgy of the Word – is proclaimed, we sing praise to God in the language of Israel:

Allelúia.

Alleluia.   *Ps. 146-150; Rev. 19:4-6*

The word *Alleluia* is a Latinized spelling of *Hallelujah*. In Hebrew, this means "Praise (*Hallelu*) Yahweh (*jah*)," or "Praise the Lord!" This is such a joyful word that, if it is not sung, it should be omitted. This word is found in several psalms; each of the last five psalms begins and ends with the word. Along with *Alleluia*, a verse from Scripture is sung which draws our attention to the Gospel reading we are about to hear.

During the season of Lent, the word *Alleluia* is not used. Instead, a penitential chant called a Tract can be used in its place, or the word can be replaced by an acclamation such as "Praise to you, Lord Jesus Christ, King of endless glory," "Glory to you, O Word of God, Lord Jesus Christ," or "Glory and praise to you, Lord Jesus Christ."

"Glory to you, O Lord."

Just before the Gospel is read, the deacon or priest says "A reading from the holy Gospel according to Matthew" (or Mark or Luke or John). We respond with:

Glória tibi, Dómine.

Glory to you, O Lord.   *Isa. 24:15; 42:12*

One reason we say this is to remember that the Gospel did not originate with the writers of the gospels (the evangelists) themselves. Rather, the Gospel is the message of God Himself which was spoken by the lips of His Son, and for that reason we give the glory to the Lord, Who will in turn bestow honor and glory and blessings upon those who do His will.

Tracing the Sign of the Cross

As we say this, we trace three small crosses on our bodies: one on our forehead, one on our lips, and one over our heart. Associated with this gesture is a silent prayer which, although not written in the Missal, has been handed on for centuries:

May the word of the Lord be in my mind,	*Phil. 4:7; Heb. 10:16*
on my lips,	*Deut. 30:14; Rom. 10:8-10*
and in my heart.	*Ps. 119:11; Ezek. 3:10; Luke 2:19*

One variant of that silent prayer is: "May the Gospel guard my mind, bless my lips, and stay in my heart." The idea is the same. The *Douay Catechism* explains the significance of this gesture this way:

> They sign themselves on their foreheads, to signify they are not, nor will be ashamed to profess Christ crucified: on their mouths to signify they will be ready with their mouths, to confess unto salvation: and on their breast to signify that with their hearts they believe unto justice. (p. 128)

This prayer reminds us of how attentive we must be to the Gospel.

Mind. We cannot let it go in one ear and out the other, it must remain in our minds. We cannot simply know *of* the Gospel, we must know the Gospel. It is not enough to know *about* Jesus Christ, we must *know* Jesus Christ, the Son of God, the Redeemer of all men. If God's Word is in our minds, it will direct our actions and give us *true* peace of mind. Remember that Christ tells us that the greatest commandment is to love God with, among other things, all our mind. (cf. Luke 10:27)

Lips. In the letter of St. James, we are told about how the tongue is a truly vicious organ:

> The tongue is a fire. The tongue is an unrighteous world among our members, staining the whole body, setting on fire the cycle of nature, and set on fire by hell. ... With it we bless the Lord and Father, and with it we curse men, who are made in the likeness of God. *From the same mouth come blessing and cursing.* My brethren, this ought not to be so. (Jas. 3:6-10)

We must guard our language carefully so as never to speak contrary to the Gospel. This means more than just avoiding blasphemy or denying Christ, this means making sure we are not false witnesses to Christ by the words we use. St. Paul exhorts the Ephesians, "Let no evil talk come out of your mouths, but only such as is good for edifying, as fits the occasion, *that it may impart grace* to those who hear." (Eph. 4:29) And to the Colossians he wrote that they should put away "anger, wrath, malice, slander, and foul talk" from their mouths. (Col. 3:8) Jesus Christ, in His Sermon on the Mount, preached that "whoever insults his brother shall be liable" to judgment. (Matt. 5:22)

Heart. A well-known psalm pleads with us not to harden our hearts when we hear the voice of the Lord. (cf. Ps. 95:8) Jesus, in His parable of the sower and the seed, refers to the seed ("the word of the kingdom") as being sown in the hearts of those who hear it. (cf. Matt. 13:19) He warns us that it is not what goes *into* a man that defiles him, but what comes out of his heart. (cf. Mark 7:18-22) We also read that the Blessed Virgin Mary, in the midst of all the commotion surrounding the birth of Jesus, "kept all these things, pondering them in her heart." (Luke 2:19) The words for "kept" and "pondering" could also be translated as "treasured" and "encountered," and this is what we are to do with the Word of God: treasure it in our hearts, not to think of it fondly every now and then, but to truly encounter it, encountering the Word.

"Praise to you, Lord Jesus Christ."

When the Gospel reading has been completed, the deacon or priest says "The Gospel of the Lord" and we respond with:

Laus tibi, Christe.

Praise to you, Lord Jesus Christ.   *Rev. 4:11; 5:12*

We give Him *glory* before we hear the Gospel, and after it we give Him *praise*. We anticipate the marvelous wonder of the Incarnation, that the Word came to dwell among us, and our response to encountering that living Word of God is to give Him praise. Glory and praise to our God!

The readings we hear from Scripture are known as *pericopes*, from the Greek word *perikope* meaning "a cutting-out" or "excerpt." You may find it helpful to prepare for Mass by reading the surrounding verses in order to get a fuller context – the *who*, *where*, and *why* – that better explains the *what* that we hear at Mass. That way, you will be able to understand them and *remember* them after they are read at Mass; the enormous benefit of reading and meditating on the Scriptures for Mass ahead of time cannot be understated.[1] You might also find it helpful to follow along with a personal missal or a "missalette" which contain the prayers and readings for the Mass, so that you can read along silently as the prayers and readings are said aloud.

The present Lectionary has a three-year cycle for Sundays and a two-year cycle for weekdays, covering almost all of the Gospels, most of the rest of the New Testament, and much of the Old Testament. On most Sundays the First Reading comes from the Old Testament, but from Easter through Pentecost, the First Reading comes from the book of Acts, in which we hear about the life and mission of the early Church. The Second Reading comes from the New Testament: either one of the letters written by St. Paul or others, or from St. John's book of Revelation.

Scripture is proclaimed at Mass not only for our benefit – our instruction and sanctification – but also for the glory of God. The readings are not only directed to *us* but also as prayers to *God*. We recount the power and marvelous deeds of God, praising Him as we grow in His wisdom. After they are proclaimed, a deacon, priest, or bishop explains them to us in the homily. Then with one voice, we stand and pray – yes, *pray* – the words of the Creed, professing our faith in the God Who has revealed Himself to us in nature, Scripture, and most perfectly, in His Son.

Questions for Reflection

1) **Interpret:** Why do we pray a psalm (or Old Testament canticle) as our response to the First Reading? Why do we retain Israel's musical heritage? Why don't we sing some other, newer song?

2) **Interpret:** Why is the Old Testament read at Mass? Why do we hear Scripture at Mass?

3) **Explain:** Why is it significant that the acclamation "The word of the Lord" is said after both the *Old* Testament reading and the *New* Testament reading?

---

[1] See the list of resources mentioned on page 19.

4) **Explain:** Why do we make the Sign of the Cross before hearing the Gospel, but not before the other readings?

5) **Explain:** The Book of the Gospels is often carried in procession at the beginning of Mass. We sing *Alleluia* before the Gospel is proclaimed. The Book can be blessed with incense. The priest makes a Sign of the Cross on it before he reads it, and he kisses the pages after he has read. The priest can be flanked by two acolytes with candles as he is reading the Gospel. Why are all these signs of reverence made to the Gospel?

6) **Relate:** How do we enter into the Scriptures proclaimed at Mass? How are they *our* story as well as that of God's chosen people?

7) **Relate:** Consider how blessed you are to be in a country where you are able to go to Mass every Sunday, where it's not against the law to practice your religion. These are things to be thankful to God for. When you say "Thanks be to God," what are you thankful for?

8) **Relate:** In the homily, the priest draws out from the Scriptures "the mysteries of faith and the rules of Christian living." (*Code of Canon Law*, can. 767 §1) How do the homilies you hear help you understand the Catholic faith and how to live out the mission of the Church in the world?

*"He professes to have knowledge of God,
and calls himself a child of the Lord."*
(Wisdom 2:13)

*Jesus said to him, "You have believed because you have seen me.
Blessed are those who have not seen and yet believe."*
(John 20:29)

7

Profession of Faith

We say a great many things in church (and out of church too) without thinking of what we are saying. For instance, we say in the Creed 'I believe in the forgiveness of sins.' I had been saying it for several years before I asked myself why it was in the Creed. At first sight it seems hardly worth putting in. 'If one is a Christian,' I thought, 'of course one believes in the forgiveness of sins. It goes without saying.' But the people who compiled the Creed apparently thought that this was a part of our belief which we needed to be reminded of every time we went to church. And I have begun to see that, as far as I am concerned, they were right. To believe in the forgiveness of sins is not nearly so easy as I thought. Real belief in it is the sort of thing that very easily slips away if we don't keep on polishing it up. (C.S. Lewis, "On Forgiveness" from *The Weight of Glory and Other Addresses*)

THE ABOVE QUOTE from C.S. Lewis (a great Anglican writer of the 20th century) speaks of a situation we all find ourselves in eventually. We've been going to Mass for quite some time, and we've prayed the Creed every week, but one day it dawns on us that we don't *quite* realize *why* we're saying it. To Lewis, the statement from the Apostles' Creed that got his attention was "the forgiveness of sins." Of course we believe sins can be and *are* forgiven! We're Christian! Christ

69

died to forgive our sins! It's such a basic concept, so who thought we needed to remind ourselves of it every week? But as Lewis points out, it's easy to *say* you believe in something (like the forgiveness of sins), but it's another to *actually believe* it is true. How many people do you know who can't forgive *themselves* of a sin, or can't forgive another person for a particular sin? Whom do *you* have trouble forgiving?

In Judaism, there is a daily recitation of a prayer known as the *Shema*, and it begins with these words: "*Shema Yisrael Adonai Eloheinu Adonai Echad!* Hear, O Israel! The LORD our God is one LORD!" (Deut. 6:4) This prayer is part of every devout Jew's daily life. In this prayer, the Jewish faith sets out, from Scripture, its basic beliefs in Who God is and what the relationship of a Jew to God should be.[1] In the Church, we do not have the *Shema*, but we have its equivalent: creeds.

The word "creed" comes from the Latin word *credo* (the first word in the Creeds), which means "I believe." Another name for a creed is a "profession of faith." When you pray the Creed, you are professing your faith by stating what it is you believe. It is also called the "symbol of faith." The word "symbol" here comes from the Greek word *symballein* which means "to put together, to synthesize." In other words, the Creed is a series of statements put together which expresses the faith of the Church and of each of her members. Creeds were most likely written up to be used as baptismal formulas: the one being baptized would give his assent to the propositions of the Creed as they were read to him, or he would say them himself. They were also used as tests of orthodoxy: only one who actually *believes* what the Creed contains would be able to say it without condemning himself.

Because the Creed is a prayer, you should avoid simply *reciting* it as you would recite the alphabet. Instead, you should make sure you know what it is you are professing to believe, so that at the end of the Creed, when you say "Amen," you can really mean it: "I give my assent to these things: I truly believe them."

The two most well-known creeds in the Catholic Church are the Apostles' Creed and the Nicene Creed. Either one of these Creeds may be used at Mass, although traditionally the Nicene Creed has been used in

---

1 The full text of the *Shema* is from Deuteronomy 6:4-9; 11:13-21 and Numbers 15:37-41.

the Roman Rite for the past thousand years, since the Creed began being used in the Roman Rite of the Mass. (The Creed has been part of other ancient liturgies since as early as the middle of the first millennium.)

Because the Creeds are lengthy, they will be broken down and explained piece by piece.

Apostles' Creed

While the Apostles' Creed is not likely to have been conceived by the Apostles themselves, it was already in existence (in almost the same form as we have it today) around A.D. 200. If you pray the Rosary or the Divine Mercy Chaplet, you are familiar with the Apostles' Creed, which is prayed at the beginning of both.

Most catechisms (e.g. the Roman Catechism of the Council of Trent, the Baltimore Catechism, the Catechism of Pope St. Pius X, and the modern Catechism) are based in part on the Apostles' Creed. The Creed is traditionally divided into twelve propositions, numbered in the English translation below. The section on the Nicene Creed will go into certain articles of faith in greater detail where it elaborates on them.

Credo in Deum Patrem omnipoténtem, Creatórem cæli et terræ,

(1) I believe in God the Father almighty,   *Gen. 17:1; Rev 16:7*
Creator of heaven and earth,   *Gen. 14:19; Acts 4:24*

This first affirmation, belief in God, is the source of every other truth: Who God is, who man is, why the world was created, what our destiny is, and so on.

God has revealed Himself as Father. We think of Him as *our* Father, but that revelation came to us through Christ: St. Paul teaches that we are *adopted* sons and daughters by being baptized into Christ and receiving the Holy Spirit. (cf. Rom. 8:15-16; Gal. 4:4-6) What is significant is that God is *eternally* the Father, which means that even before He created us or anything else, He was already Father. This implies the "plurality of persons" in God: if God, before anything or anyone was created, could rightly be called "Father," there must have been Someone (also eternal, and also God) of Whom He was the Father.

We use many adjectives to describe God: merciful, loving, wise, etc. We profess in the Creed that God is unlimited in power, omnipotent.

God is most frequently referred to as almighty, and from the boundlessness of His might flows His other attributes: God cannot be both almighty and lacking fullness of wisdom, for example.

God the Father creates by the power of His Word: "And God said..." (Gen. 1:3) God created both the heavens (the spiritual realm and all therein) and the earth (meaning the material, physical world). God created the entire universe, *ex nihilo* (out of nothing; cf. 2 Macc. 7:28; Rom. 4:17). This means that God was before all things and that there is no thing that God did not make (cf. John 1:3), not that God cannot (or does not) use pre-existing matter that He *first* created to *further* create things: God formed Adam, not out of thin air, but "of dust from the ground." (Gen. 2:7)

**et in Iesum Christum, Fílium eius únicum, Dóminum nostrum,
qui concéptus est de Spíritu Sancto, natus ex María Vírgine,
passus sub Póntio Piláto, crucifíxus, mórtuus, et sepúltus,**

» **(2)** and in Jesus Christ, his only Son, our Lord,   *John 1:14; Phil. 2:11*
» **(3)** who was conceived by the Holy Spirit,   *Matt. 1:18-20*
» born of the Virgin Mary,   *Luke 1:30-35*
» **(4)** suffered under Pontius Pilate,   *Matt. 27:27-30; John 19:1-3*
   was crucified,   *Matt. 27:35; Acts 2:36; 1 Cor. 2:8*
   died and was buried;   *Matt. 27:50-60; Rom. 5:6; 1 Cor. 15:3*

The next six propositions (these three and the next three) condense the Gospel into a few short phrases. These three cover the identity of Jesus, the manner of His conception and birth, and the circumstances of His Passion.

We know the name "Jesus" means "*YHWH* saves." The word "Christ" is not His surname (as if His foster father was Joseph Christ). The Greek word *Christos* is the translation of the Hebrew word *Moshiach* which means "anointed [one]." Jesus was not the only figure in Scripture identified as God's anointed one – Israel's prophets, priests, and kings were all anointed with oil as a sign of their having been chosen by God for a particular mission. Even pagans, such as Cyrus the King of Persia, were identified by God as "his anointed." (Isa. 45:1) But Jesus is the true Messiah, the true Christ; His anointing was unlike any other.

Jesus, the eternal Son of God, is called the Father's *only* Son. The Nicene Creed clarifies this point: Jesus is the only *begotten* Son of God;

we are sons and daughters by adoption through the Holy Spirit. Jesus is also called *Lord*, which indicates His divinity. We call Jesus Lord because He is our Redeemer from sin and death. (cf. Phil. 2:6-11)

The Son of God was conceived *temporally* by the Holy Spirit in the womb of the Blessed Virgin Mary, from whom He took His flesh. This mystery of faith is called the Incarnation. By means of this real human body, Jesus, the Son of God, endured suffering and, ultimately, death. By mentioning Pontius Pilate, the Creed places the earthly existence of Jesus in a specific period of history.

At the words "who was conceived ... of the Virgin Mary" (*"qui conceptus ... ex Maria Virgine"*) we make a profound bow of the body[2] in reverence to this most wondrous mystery of the Incarnation.

descéndit ad ínferos, tértia die resurréxit a mórtuis,
ascéndit ad cælos, sedet ad déxteram Dei Patris omnipoténtis,
inde ventúrus est iudicáre vivos et mórtuos.

» **(5)** he descended into hell;	*Rom. 10:7; Eph. 4:9-10; 1 Pet. 3:18-19*
on the third day	*Luke 24:46; Acts 10:40; 1 Cor. 15:4*
he rose again from the dead;	*Rom 4:25-26; 1 Th. 4:14; 1 Pet. 1:12*
(6) he ascended into heaven,	*Mark 16:19; Luke 24:51; Rom. 10:6*
and is seated at the right hand	*Luke 22:69; Acts 7:55; Rom 8:34*
» of God the Father almighty;	
» **(7)** from there he will come	*Matt. 25:31; 1 Th. 4:16; 2 Th. 1:9-10*
to judge the living and the dead.	*Acts 10:42; 2 Tim. 4:1; 1 Pet. 4:5*

These three propositions cover the result of Christ's death: His descent into the abode of the dead, His Resurrection and Ascension, and His future coming in glory.

The Latin word *inferos* (translated as "hell") is not the Hell of the damned, but rather the abode of the souls of the dead, known in Hebrew as *Sheol*. The human soul of Christ, united to His divine Person, was in this "hell" while His human body (also united to His divine Person) lay in the tomb. (cf. *Catechism* 630) On the third day, His body and soul were reunited by the power of His divinity, rising anew ("again"), to a new glorified life.

---

[2] On the Annunciation of Our Lord (March 25) and the Nativity of Our Lord (December 25), we genuflect instead of bow.

73

After forty days, during which He appeared to His disciples, Jesus ascended into Heaven and took His place at the Father's right hand. He will return at the end of time to carry out the final (general) judgment.

Credo in Spíritum Sanctum, sanctam Ecclésiam cathólicam, Sanctórum communiónem, remissiónem peccatórum, carnis resurrectiónem, vitam ætérnam. Amen.

(8) I believe in the Holy Spirit,   *John 14:26; Acts 2:4; 2 Cor. 13:14*
(9) the holy catholic Church,   *Acts 9:31; Eph. 5:27*
the communion of saints,   *Acts 2:44; Heb. 12:1-2,22-24; 1 John 1:3; 2 John 1:1*
(10) the forgiveness of sins,   *John 20:23; Acts 2:38; Eph. 1:7*
(11) the resurrection of the body,   *2 Macc. 7; John 5:29; Rom. 6:5; 1 Cor. 15*
» **(12)** and life everlasting. Amen.   *Dan. 12:2; John 17:3; 1 John 5:20; Jude 1:21*

The last part of the Creed deals with several propositions which, at first, might appear unrelated. They are, in fact, related to the first of these five articles of faith, the Holy Spirit: Who is the third Person of the Trinity; Who forms and gives life to the Church, and Who unites all her members in communion; by Whom Christ gave His Apostles the power to forgive sins; Who restores our bodies in the resurrection; and Who fills us with new and eternal life.

Nicene Creed

Most Catholics are probably more familiar with the Nicene Creed.[3] This Creed was written (in two stages) in the 4th century to combat a few heresies, the most serious of which was Arianism, named for its chief proponent, Arius. Arius was a bishop who believed that the Son of God was not co-eternal with the Father, but was a creation, so He could not be considered "God," and so was *not* worthy of worship and adoration. The Creed's language defines and defends the orthodox Catholic faith. It is not *exhaustive* – you will notice only one sacrament is mentioned, Baptism – but it is *certain*.

In 1968, Pope Paul VI wrote an Apostolic Letter known as the *Credo of the People of God*. This was an elaboration and explanation of the Creed

---

[3] The Nicene Creed is properly called the Nicene-Constantinopolitan Creed, because it was developed in two stages: first at the Council of Nicaea in A.D. 325, and then at the Council of Constantinople in A.D. 381. The Constantinopolitan revision primarily affected the latter part of the Creed, adding the words following "And in the Holy Spirit." The Creed was later revised in A.D. 589 at the Third Council of Toledo to include the word *Filioque*.

which included beliefs such as original sin, the identity of the Catholic Church (governed by the successor of St. Peter) with the "one, holy, catholic, and apostolic Church," transubstantiation, and Purgatory. His letter is an excellent guide to understanding the Creed more completely.

**Credo in unum Deum, Patrem omnipoténtem,
factórem cæli et terræ, visibílium ómnium et invisibílium.**

» I believe in one God, the Father almighty,   *Dan. 3:45; 1 Tim. 2:5*
  maker of heaven and earth,   *Gen. 14:19; Acts 17:24*
» of all things visible and invisible.   *Wis. 1:14; Col. 1:16; Rev. 4:11*

I Believe

Before we look at the first part of the Nicene Creed, we should look at the first *word*, because this has been changed in the new translation. The Latin word *credo* means "I believe" (whereas *credimus* means "we believe"). The old English translation began with "We believe." The Latin text has not changed; rather, the translation is now accurate: we begin by saying "*I* believe."

Why the change? The 2001 instruction on the proper translation of liturgical texts explains the reason for the use of the first person singular:

> The Creed is to be translated according to the precise wording that the tradition of the Latin Church has bestowed upon it, including the use of the first person singular, by which is clearly made manifest that "the confession of faith is handed down in the Creed, as it were, *as coming from the person of the whole Church*, united by means of the Faith." (*Liturgiam Authenticam* 65)

During the Confiteor (and later when you say "Lord, I am not worthy…" before Communion) you are speaking for yourself as one imperfect and sinful member of the Church. Here, however, all the faithful, with one voice, are speaking as the Church, the single spotless spouse of Christ whose faith is perfect. (cf. *Catechism* 167)

One God

While the Apostles' Creed begins with belief *in God*, the Nicene Creed clarifies this as belief in *one* God. This establishes two things: first, that the same God created both the heavens (the spiritual realm) and the earth (the visible realm); second, that the Father, the Son, and the Holy Spirit are *each* God but are not *three* Gods.

Father and Creator

Along with the identity of Father comes a sense of Creator (origin of all things) and Ruler (governor and preserver of all things). In addition to being the source of all created things, God the Father is the source of the Godhead, the divine substance. (cf. *Catechism* 245) At the Council of Toledo XI (A.D. 675), it was explained in this way:

> We confess and believe ... that the Father, indeed, is not begotten, not created but unbegotten. For He from whom both the Son received His nativity and the Holy Spirit His procession takes His origin from no one. Therefore, He is the source and origin of all Godhead. (*Denzinger* 525.2)

The Son is begotten by the Father, and the Spirit proceeds from the Father (and the Son), but the Father is the source of the divine essence: He does not get it by being begotten by, nor by proceeding from, some other "father" before Him.

Visible and Invisible

Where we once used the words "seen and unseen," we now say "visible and invisible." By saying *visible*, we mean all of physical creation, even that which is visible but yet unseen by us (like the farthest reaches of space), and by *invisible*, we mean all the spiritual realm, even that which sometimes manifests itself to us in ways we can detect, even with our eyes. The invisible includes, first and foremost, angels and souls.

The belief that the *same* God created both the physical and the spiritual attacks one of the early heresies which plagued the Church, Gnosticism (and specifically, Manichaeism). The Gnostic viewpoint generally considered the flesh and all material, physical things as evil (as opposed to "good" and "very good" as God declares them in Genesis 1), the product of an evil god, while the spiritual and non-corporeal things were created by a good god. To advance this heresy, the Gnostics taught that the god of the Old Testament was an evil corruptor who captured pure spiritual beings in bodies of flesh and subjected them to laws and statutes, and that Jesus defeated this demon and revealed the true god in the New Testament.

The faith of the Church, contrary to the Gnostic heresy, testifies that the God Who revealed Himself to Israel and the God Whom Jesus revealed to His disciples are *one and the same God*. This means that there is a unity in the Scriptures, because this one God is the divine Author of both the Old and New Testaments. This one God created everything that is, and St. Paul testified that Jesus, the Son of God,

> is the image of the invisible God, the first-born of all creation; for *in him all things were created*, in heaven and on earth, visible and invisible, whether thrones or dominions or principalities or authorities – *all things were created through him and for him*. He is before all things, and in him all things hold together. (Col. 1:15-17)

Et in unum Dóminum Iesum Christum, Fílium Dei Unigénitum, et ex Patre natum ante ómnia sǽcula.

» And in one Lord Jesus Christ,	*Deut. 6:4; 1 Cor. 8:6; Eph. 4:5*
» the Only Begotten Son of God,	*Ps. 2:7; John 1:14; Heb. 1:5*
» born of the Father before all ages.	*Col. 1:15-17; 1 Pet. 1:20; Jude 1:25*

The Apostles' Creed does not explain the eternal origins of Jesus. The Nicene Creed, to combat the Arian heresy, makes this very clear so as to remove all doubt.

The first thing we need to understand is why the Creed uses the word "begotten" and expressly avoids the word "created." The verb *beget* is traditionally used of a father, and it means "to father a child." God the Father begat God the Son. It is not the same as creating. A father begets a child who is of the same nature and substance as the father: man begets man, horse begets horse. A man *creates* something unlike him in nature and substance: man creates a statue, a car, a house.

Because the Father *begat* the Son, that means the Son is of the same nature and substance as the Father: the Son is divine like the Father is divine, and because the Son is divine and the nature of divinity is eternal, the Father begat the Son *eternally*. If the Father had *created* the Son, the Son would not – *could* not – be divine, could not be God, because God is uncreated and eternal, and created things have an origin in time. We can't really fathom it, but here is the first amazing mystery of the Trinity: the Father begat the Son eternally, so there was no time (since time did not even exist yet) before the Father begat the Son: the Father was never without the Son. This is what we mean when we say "born of the Father before all ages," or, as we used to say, "eternally begotten of the Father." *We*, on the other hand, were not begotten by God, we were *created* by God. God begets eternally, He creates temporally. We are not His begotten children, we are His created and adopted children. Jesus is the Son of God by *nature* and we are sons and daughters of God by *grace*. This is why we confess Jesus as the only *begotten* Son of God.

Deum de Deo, lumen de lúmine, Deum verum de Deo vero, génitum, non factum, consubstantiálem Patri: per quem ómnia facta sunt.

God from God,	*Luke 1:35; Phil. 2:6-7*
Light from Light,	*Luke 2:32; John 1:4-9; 1 John 1:5; Rev. 21:23*
true God from true God,	*Ex. 3:14; John 8:24,28,58*
» begotten, not made, consubstantial with the Father;	*Col. 1:19; Heb. 1:3*
through him all things were made.	*John 1:3; Col. 1:15-16; Heb. 1:2*

The Nicene Creed seeks to make clear that Jesus, God the Son, is *in no way* inferior in divinity to God the Father. In teaching that Jesus is "God from God" the Church professes that God begets God, so the Son is as much God as the Father Who begot Him. By extension, "true God from true God" means that the Father and the Son are *completely* and *truly* God, not partially God (as if such a thing could be). The phrase "Light from Light" can use some more elaboration.

Light from Light

From Scripture, we know that "God is light" (1 John 1:5) and that the Word of God (Jesus, the Son) is "the true light." (John 1:8-9) Simeon, a Jewish prophet who lived to see the birth of Jesus, called Him "a light for revelation to the Gentiles" (Luke 2:32), and Jesus revealed himself on many occasions to be "the light of the world." (John 8:12; 9:5; 12:46) The experience of Saul on the road to Damascus was of "a light from heaven" from which the voice of Jesus came. (Acts 9:3) So when we say that Jesus is "light from light," we are affirming that just as God the Father is Light and Jesus comes from the Father, Jesus is Light. This doctrine was defended eloquently in the 4th century by St. Hilary.

St. Hilary (c. A.D. 300 – c. 368), Bishop of Poitiers and a Doctor of the Church, was known as "the Athanasius[4] of the West" and as the "Hammer of Arius." In addition to fighting the Arian heresy, he wrote a twelve-book work on the Trinity. In Book VI, he addresses and corrects

---

[4] St. Athanasius was the bishop of Alexandria (in Egypt) who stood up to Arius at the First Council of Nicaea and defended the orthodox Catholic faith concerning the divinity of Christ.

various heretical claims that the Son of God is a created being. These claims *looked* orthodox at first glance, but St. Hilary showed that they twisted the language of the Church to advance their own interpretation. One pseudo-creed includes a clause denying that the Son is "a light from a light, or a lamp with two flames," a belief attributed to an Egyptian named Hieracas. This clause denies both a truth (that the Son *is* "light from light") and a heresy (that the relation of the Son to the Father is *not* like "a lamp with two flames").

St. Hilary wrote:

> Hieracas ... talks of two flames from one lamp. This symmetrical pair of flames, fed by the supply of oil contained in one bowl, is His illustration of the substance of Father and Son. It is as though that substance were something *separate* from Either Person, like the oil in the lamp, which is distinct from the two flames, though they depend upon it for their existence. ... But the true faith asserts that God is born from God, as light from light, which pours itself forth without self-diminution, giving what it has yet having what it gave. (*De Trinitate*, VI, 12)

First he describes the problem with the theory of "two flames from one lamp." If the Father and the Son are two flames which draw from a common supply of oil, that means that the Father is *not* the source of the Son, but simply a co-dependent *with* the Son on some source (the oil). He counters this with the Church's faith, that God (the Father) begets God (the Son) as light "pours itself forth" without being reduced or losing anything of itself, "*giving* what it *has* yet *having* what it *gave*." He continues by saying that the faith of the Church asserts that

> They Two [Father and Son] are One, for He [the Father], from Whom He [the Son] is born, is as Himself [having no source], and He that was born [the Son] has neither another source nor another nature [other than the Father], for He [the Son] is Light from Light. (*Ibid.*)

In other words, the source of the Son is none other than the Father, and so the Son has the same nature as the Father, as light from light.

St. Hilary then laments that the authors of this pseudo-creed are putting this false two-flame theory in the mouths "of those who confess Light from Light" in an attempt to draw people away from the faith of the Church. Finally, he contrasts once more the two-flame theory with the Church's belief, explaining that the Church does not believe the Son is a "prolongation" or "extension" or "continuation" of the Father, but is truly begotten of the Father:

> [T]he unchangeable God begat God. Their bond of union is not, like that of two flames, two wicks of one lamp, something outside Themselves. The birth of the Only-begotten Son from God is not a prolongation in space, but a begetting; not an extension, but Light from Light. For the unity of light with light is a unity of nature, not unbroken continuation. (*Ibid.*)

That is what we mean when we say that Jesus, the Son, is "light from light."

Consubstantial

In the old translation, we said "*one in being* with the Father," but now we say "*consubstantial* with the Father." It is not that the old translation was wrong, but the new translation is more accurate (more faithful to the Latin). The word "consubstantial" comes straight from the Latin word *consubstantialem*, made up of two parts, *con-* (with, joint) and *substantia* (substance); it is a translation of the Greek term *homoousios* which is also made up of two parts, *homo-* (same) and *ousia* (essence, being).[5] We say that the Son is of the same substance or essence as the Father: They are one in substance. In order to understand "substance" and "essence" we need to know a bit more about the underlying language.

What does "substance" mean? If we look at it in Latin, we have *sub-* (under) and *stantia* (to stand). In Catholic theological terminology, the *substance* of a thing is what "stands under" its form or appearance. For example, we say that the bread and wine are transubstantiated into the Body, Blood, Soul, and Divinity of Jesus Christ; they are not *transformed*, because the visible form (the appearance of the bread and wine) does not change, but the *substance*, that which stands beneath the visible form, changes. In modern language, the "substance" of a thing is that which the thing *really is*. Our individual substance, who we are, does not change even though our outer form changes as we develop and age.

What does "essence" mean? It is related to the word "essential." If some characteristic is *essential* to an object, it means that object cannot *be*

---

[5] The word *homoousios* ("of the same substance") is not to be confused with *homoiousios* ("of similar substance") which differs by a single *iota* (the Greek letter *i*). These two words were the subject of much debate at the First Council of Nicaea.

that object without that characteristic. For example, no matter what a chair looks like, it is essential that a chair can be sat in. The Latin verb for "to be" is *esse*. The "*essence*" of a thing is that which makes the thing *be* itself. If that sounds a lot like "substance," it should.

Jesus, God the Son, is not "one in being" with the Father as if the Son and the Father are *the same being*, the same Person. The Persons of the Trinity are distinct Persons: the Father is not the Son, the Son is not the Holy Spirit, and the Holy Spirit is not the Father. Rather, the Son and the Father share the same substance, because there is only *one* divine substance. The Father, the Son, and the Holy Spirit are *of the same (divine) substance*, not just a similar substance. They are not just vaguely like each other, they are specifically of the same substance. Arius did not believe that; he believed that the Son was a *creation*, and a creation cannot share in the substance of the one who created it. That is why we repeat again in the Creed, "begotten, not made."

**Qui propter nos hómines et propter nostram salútem
descéndit de cælis.
Et incarnátus est de Spíritu Sancto
ex María Vírgine, et homo factus est.**

For us men and for our salvation,	*Matt. 1:21; Acts 4:12; 2 Tim. 2:10*
he came down from heaven,	*John 6:38; 16:28; 1 Cor. 15:47*
» and by the Holy Spirit was incarnate	*Luke 1:30-35; John 1:14*
» of the Virgin Mary, and became man.	*Gal. 4:4; Matt. 1:18-20; Luke 24:39*

Up to this point, the Nicene Creed has explained the divine nature and eternal nativity of Jesus. Here the Creed deals with His human nature and temporal nativity, and the *reason* for it.

God came down from Heaven and assumed a true human nature "for us men and for our salvation." God the Son, unchanged in His divinity, assumed our human nature – flesh, blood, soul, and will – so as to be "made like his brethren *in every respect*" and "who in every respect has been tempted as we are, *yet without sinning*." (Heb. 2:17; 4:15) Jesus, without losing His divinity, took on humanity in perfection. St. John describes this in the opening chapter of his gospel: "the Word became flesh." (John 1:14) This "becoming flesh" is described by the word "incarnate" which means "in the flesh" (*in-* + *carne*).

Incarnate

The man Jesus was not conceived like other men, but by the Holy Spirit in the virginal womb of Mary, who retained her virginity before, during, and after the birth of Jesus. Jesus took His flesh and blood from His mother, Mary. At the very instant of His conception, Jesus was God and man in perfection, and His human soul was instantly filled with the Holy Spirit. The Incarnation is such an important mystery of the faith that at the words "and by the Holy Spirit... became man" ("*et incarnatus ... homo factus est*") we make a profound bow of the body[6] in reverence.

In the old translation of the Creed, the phrase "*incarnatus est*" was translated as "he was *born*" instead of "he was *incarnate*." By saying "he was born (*natus est*) of the Virgin Mary and became man," one might assume that He only "became man" at His birth. This is contrary to the true text of the Creed, and also to the faith of the Church concerning the humanity of the unborn: at the moment of conception, there is a living human being, a person. Jesus became man at the moment He received His flesh, at His conception, *not* at His birth.

The dual natures in Jesus often lead to confusion about Who (or rather, how *many* Who's) Jesus is. He is not *two* Sons, but *one* Son with an eternal nativity by the Father, and a temporal nativity by the Blessed Virgin Mary. He is not *two* Persons, but *one* Divine Person, not a human person; this is why we say He "became man" and not "became a person," because He already was a Person. He does have *two* natures and *two* wills, divine and human. As a man, He has a body and a soul and a will. The Catechism quotes the Council of Chalcedon in A.D. 451 which explained in great detail the completeness of the two natures of Jesus:

> Following the holy Fathers, we unanimously teach and confess one and the same Son, our Lord Jesus Christ: the same perfect in divinity and perfect in humanity, the same truly God and truly man, composed of rational soul and body; consubstantial with the Father as to his divinity and consubstantial with us as to his humanity; "like us in all things but sin." He was begotten from the Father before all ages as to his divinity and in these last days, for us and for our salvation, was born as to his humanity of the virgin Mary, the Mother of God. We confess that one and the

---

[6] On the Annunciation of Our Lord (March 25) and the Nativity of Our Lord (December 25), we genuflect instead of bow.

same Christ, Lord, and only-begotten Son, is to be acknowledged in two natures without confusion, change, division or separation. (*Catechism* 467, quoting *Denzinger* 301-302; cf. Heb. 4:15)

Mary, the Mother of God

A woman who gives birth to a boy is the origin of the boy's body, but not his soul (which comes from God), even though the boy's human nature consists of both body and soul. To say that she is the mother of the boy does not mean she is the origin of the boy's soul or his complete nature, but that she is the mother of the whole *person*.

Because Jesus is God, and Mary is the mother of Jesus and gave birth to Him, the Church rightly professes that Mary is the Mother of God (and the *Theotokos*, the God-Bearer, as she is called in the Eastern Churches). This does not mean that Mary is divine or that she preceded God or is His source or origin. It simply means that since the human nature of Jesus cannot be separated from His divine nature, and Mary gave birth to the *whole* Jesus, Mary is Mother of God. Mary is the Mother of God because a woman is the mother of a *person*, not a *nature*.

Crucifíxus étiam pro nobis sub Póntio Piláto;
passus et sepúltus est, et resurréxit tértia die, secúndum Scriptúras,
et ascéndit in cælum, sedet ad déxteram Patris.

For our sake he was crucified under Pontius Pilate,	*Mark 15:15; Acts 2:36*
» he suffered death and was buried,	*Matt. 27:50-60; Rom. 5:6*
» and rose again on the third day	*Luke 9:22; 24:46; Acts 10:40*
» in accordance with the Scriptures.	*Luke 24:27; Acts 18:28; 1 Cor. 15:3-4*
He ascended into heaven	*Luke 24:51; Rom. 10:6; 1 Tim. 3:16*
and is seated at the right hand of the Father.	*Luke 22:69; Rom 8:34*

The Nicene Creed expands slightly the description of the Passion and death of Christ. While it omits the part about Jesus descending to hell, it is important to remember that both the Apostles' Creed and the Nicene Creed teach the truth, and just because one Creed omits what another includes does not mean that one denies the other.

Here the Nicene Creed adopts the language of St. Paul, professing that Christ's Passion, death, and Resurrection happened "in accordance with the Scriptures." (1 Cor. 15:3-4) Also note the following change: in the old translation, we said that Jesus "*suffered, died, and was buried*," but now we say He "*suffered death* and was buried." The Latin and Greek texts use a single verb (*passus* in Latin, *pathonta* in Greek) which indicates a suffering demise.

Seated at the Right Hand of the Father

In the creeds (as in the *Gloria*) we say that Jesus is "*seated* at the *right hand* of the Father*." While Jesus does indeed have a body of flesh and blood, we are not speaking about a physical position – remember that Stephen saw Christ *standing* at God's right hand (cf. Acts 7:55-56) – nor about a physical hand of God the Father Who is Spirit.

Making an analogy from human affairs to divine ones, the Roman Catechism explains that "[a]s among men he who sits at the right hand is considered to occupy the most honorable place, so, transferring the same idea to celestial things, to express the glory which Christ as man has obtained above all others, we confess that He sits at the right hand of the Father." (Creed, VI) We are affirming that Jesus is at the Father's right hand not *only* in His divinity but *also* in His humanity; he is "equal to his Father in power and majesty." (*Douay Catechism*, p. 17) Scripture speaks of God's right hand as being "glorious in power" and "shatter[ing] the enemy" (Ex. 15:6), and it is from His right hand that He dispenses all His good gifts. (cf. Ps. 16:11) This means that Christ shares in the power, glory, and victory of His Father. (cf. Rev. 5:13; *Catechism* 663)

The Constitution on the Sacred Liturgy explains that we participate, on earth, in the heavenly liturgy "where Christ is sitting at the right hand of God, a minister of the holies and of the true tabernacle." (CSL 8, cf. Heb. 8:1-2) Jesus' place at the Father's right hand is explained in liturgical terms in the letter to the Hebrews. It was after "he had made purification for sins" that Christ "sat down at the right hand of the Majesty on high" (Heb. 1:3), a position that the Father has never even shared with the angels. (cf. Heb. 1:13) Jesus is there as our "high priest" (Heb. 8:1), and a visual distinction is made between the priests of the Temple who *stand* day after day in their service, and Jesus, *seated* at the right hand of God, who offered Himself once and for all. Describing Jesus as sitting rather than standing shows that His priesthood surpasses that of the Mosaic covenant.

But again, this description of Jesus being seated "does not imply here position and posture of body, but expresses the firm and permanent possession of royal and supreme power and glory which He received from the Father." (*Roman Catechism*, Creed, VI) Jesus is not resting at His Father's side, but continually interceding on our behalf. (cf. Heb. 7:25)

Finally, the entrance of Christ into Heaven, taking His place at the right hand of His Father, "signifies the inauguration of the Messiah's kingdom, the fulfillment of the prophet Daniel's vision concerning the Son of man: 'To him was given dominion and glory and kingdom, that all peoples, nations, and languages should serve him; his dominion is an everlasting dominion, which shall not pass away, and his kingdom one that shall not be destroyed.' (Dan. 7:14)" (*Catechism* 664) This kingdom, which is present on earth through the Church, is the subject of the next part of the Creed:

Et íterum ventúrus est cum glória, iudicáre vivos et mórtuos, cuius regni non erit finis.

He will come again in glory	*Matt. 25:31; 1 Th. 4:16; 2 Th. 1:9-10*
to judge the living and the dead	*Acts 10:42; 2 Tim. 4:1; 1 Pet. 4:5*
and his kingdom will have no end.	*Dan. 2:4; 7:14; Luke 1:33; 2 Pet. 1:11*

The Nicene Creed describes the second coming of Christ as glorious, as the Lord himself says: the glory in which the Son returns is both "the glory of his Father" (Matt. 16:27) and "his glory." (Matt. 25:31) The Creed also mentions the everlasting kingdom of Jesus as described in Daniel 7:14 and Luke 1:33. The reign of God has no end. We celebrate this reign in a special way on the Solemnity of Christ, King of the Universe.

St. John explains how we are members of this kingdom: Jesus "has freed us from our sins by his blood and made us a kingdom, priests to his God and Father." (Rev. 1:6; cf. Rev. 5:10) The victory of Jesus, by His crucifixion and resurrection, over Satan shows that "[n]ow the salvation and the power and the kingdom of our God and the authority of his Christ have come." (Rev. 12:10)

The Living and the Dead

The phrase "the living and the dead" can generally be interpreted in two ways. First, that there may very well be men still living at the time of Christ's return, and that they will not die before the judgment. Second, that "the living" refers to those to be rewarded with "everlasting life"

(Dan. 12:2) in the "resurrection of life" (John 5:29) and "of the just" (Luke 14:14), and that "the dead" refers to those to be condemned with "shame and everlasting contempt" (Dan. 12:2) and spiritual death in the "resurrection of judgment." (John 5:29)

Et in Spíritum Sanctum, Dóminum et vivificántem:
qui ex Patre Filióque procédit.
Qui cum Patre et Fílio simul adorátur et conglorificátur:
qui locútus est per prophétas.

» And in the Holy Spirit, the Lord, *Gen. 1:2; 2 Cor. 3:17-18*
the giver of life, *Gen. 2:7; Job 33:4; Rom. 8:2; 2 Cor. 3:6*
who proceeds from the Father *John 14:26; Acts 2:1-4; Rom. 8:9*
and the Son, *John 15:26; 16:7; John 20:22; Rom. 8:9*
» who with the Father and the Son is adored and glorified, *2 Cor. 13:14*
» who has spoken through the prophets. *2 Sam. 23:2; Heb. 3:7; 2 Pet. 1:21*

The elaboration on the Person of the Holy Spirit was formulated at the Council of Constantinople in A.D. 381. The Creed confirms the divinity of the Holy Spirit, His origin, and His actions.

By calling the Holy Spirit "Lord" the Church does not believe there are two Lords, Jesus and the Holy Spirit, but only one Lord. Just as she teaches that there is one God in three Persons (and not three Gods), so too she teaches that the one Lord is three Persons as well: Father, Son, and Holy Spirit. In affirming that the Holy Spirit is Lord, we profess that He is not a *created* spirit like an angel, but that He is uncreated Spirit. By adoring and glorifying the Holy Spirit with the Father and the Son, we further confess that the Holy Spirit is God (Who alone is worthy of adoration).

The Holy Spirit is the vivifier, the animator, the "giver of life." The Spirit gives life, first and foremost, to humanity and to the Church. The Spirit unites our souls to God Who is the true source of our life. It was not until God "breathed" into Adam the "breath of life" that he became "a living soul." (Gen. 2:7) The Hebrew word for Spirit is *ruah*, the same word for "wind" and "breath."

To the Holy Spirit is attributed the "inspiration" of the prophets. To *inspire* is to *breathe into*, and since the Spirit is seen as the "breath" of God, the imagery is quite appropriate. The letter to the Hebrews begins by affirming that God spoke in times past "by the prophets." (Heb. 1:1)

St. Peter said that "the Holy Spirit spoke beforehand by the mouth of David." (Acts 1:16; cf. Acts 4:24-25) He also described the true origin of prophecy in this way: "no prophecy ever came by the impulse of man, but men moved by the Holy Spirit spoke from God." (2 Pet. 1:21) In numerous places in the New Testament, a person is said to be "filled with the Holy Spirit" and then proclaim prophetic words: St. John the Baptist (cf. Luke 1:15), his parents Sts. Elizabeth and Zechariah (cf. Luke 1:41ff, 67ff), the disciples at Pentecost (cf. Acts 2:4), Sts. Peter and John (cf. Acts 4:8, 31), and St. Paul. (cf. Acts 13:9ff)

Filioque ("and the Son")

The Creed, as written in A.D. 381, stated that the Holy Spirit "proceeds from the Father." This is absolutely true. What is *also* true is the addition of the word *Filioque*, which was later added to prevent the statement that the Holy Spirit "proceeds from the Father" from being misinterpreted. The addition of this one word has caused much controversy between the Western Church (which added the word) and the Eastern Church.[7]

The word *Filioque* was added less than two centuries later, as it appears in the proceedings of the Third Council of Toledo in A.D. 589. Whether it was in use before that date is uncertain, but explicit doctrinal support precedes that Council. To understand the belief that the Holy Spirit proceeds from *both* the Father *and* the Son, we should look at the Scriptural and Patristic evidence.

The Gospel according to St. John describes the relationship between the three Persons thoroughly: the Son has received everything from the Father (cf. 3:35); the Father will send the Counselor, "the Spirit of truth" (14:16-17) in the name of the Son (cf. 14:26); the Son shall send the Spirit from the Father (cf. 15:26); and Jesus *breathes* the Spirit upon the Apostles to give them the power to forgive or retain sins. (cf. 20:22) St. Paul calls the Holy Spirit the Spirit both "of God" and "of Christ." (Rom. 8:9)

St. Ambrose (A.D. c. 340 – 397), Bishop of Milan and a very important Latin Church Father, wrote quite plainly in his work on the Holy Spirit (*De Spiritu Sancto*, I, 11) that the Spirit "proceeds from the Son" (*procedit ex Filio*) and "proceeds from the Father and the Son"

---

[7] It should be noted that Eastern Rites in communion with the Roman See (that is, Eastern *Catholic* Rites) recite the Creed as composed in A.D. 381, without saying "and the Son."

(*procedit a Patre et Filio*). His protégé, St. Augustine (A.D. 354 – 430), equal if not greater in influence, began a lengthy work in several books on the Trinity around A.D. 400, which was not published until around A.D. 416. Near the end of the last book, he explains that as there is no "time" in God, you cannot say that the Son was begotten *first* and *then* the Holy Spirit proceeded: there is no "first" and "second" in eternity. Furthermore, the Spirit cannot be said to proceed *twice* (once from the Father, and then again from the Father *and* the Son) since there is no repetition in eternity. In the end, St. Augustine declares it a mystery:

> [L]et him who can understand the generation of the Son from the Father without time, understand also the procession of the Holy Spirit *from both* without time. ... [T]he Holy Spirit proceeds from the Father principally, the Father giving the procession without any interval of time, yet in common from both [the Father and the Son]. (*De Trinitate*, IV, 26, 47)

Pope St. Leo I taught in A.D. 447 that the Holy Spirit proceeds from both Father and Son in his letter *Quam laudabiliter* (cf. *Catechism* 247, *Denzinger* 284) where he states that the Trinity is made up of "the One Who begets, the Other Who was begotten, the Other Who proceeded from *both*" (*de* utroque *processit*). The same Latin expression (although in a different tense) was used by Augustine above: "*de utroque procedit.*"

Et unam, sanctam, cathólicam et apostólicam Ecclésiam.
Confíteor unum baptísma in remissiónem peccatórum.
Et exspécto resurrectiónem mortuórum,
et vitam ventúri sǽculi. Amen.

» And one, holy, catholic, and apostolic Church. *Eph. 2:14-20; 4:4-6; 5:27*
» I confess one baptism for the forgiveness of sins *Acts 2:38; 22:16; Eph. 4:5*
» and I look forward to the resurrection of the dead *2 Macc. 12:43; Rom. 6:5*
   and the life of the world to come. Amen. *Dan. 12:2; Rev. 21:1,27*

The end of the Creed covers the Church, baptism and forgiveness, the resurrection, and eternal life. The Creed describes the Church more fully, and we will look at those four "marks" in detail. The forgiveness of sins is expressly linked to *one* baptism. The resurrection is said to be "of the dead" whereas the Apostles' Creed used the phrase "of the body" (literally, "of the flesh"); this is not a change in belief, but it may lead to thinking that the *body* is not raised, so it deserves explanation.

The Church

The word "church" comes from the Greek *ekklesia*, meaning "assembly" or "congregation." More basically, it means "those called out," from the roots *ek-* (out) and *kaleo* (to call). But what is it we were called out of? We are called out of darkness and sin, as St. Peter tells us: "you are a chosen race, a royal priesthood, a holy nation, God's own people, that you may declare the wonderful deeds of him who *called you out of darkness* into his marvelous light." (1 Pet. 2:9) The Creed describes this Church, this assembly of those whom God has called out of darkness, as **one, holy, catholic,** and **apostolic.** These four "marks" of the Church all come from Scripture and identify the Church which was founded by Jesus Christ.

One. Jesus founded only *one* Church; He said to St. Peter "I will build my *Church*" (Matt. 16:18), not *churches*. Because the Church is the body of Christ (cf. Eph. 5:23; Col. 1:18), and Christ has only *one* body, the Church must also be one. St. Paul teaches that we are called into one Church, one body. (cf. Eph. 4:4; Col. 3:15) This *one* Church also has only *one* faith. (cf. Eph. 4:5; Jude 1:3) Jesus prayed that all His disciples would "be one" as He and the Father are one. (cf. John 17:22-23) The Church has *one* head, even though that head is both invisible (Christ himself) and visible (the Pope, successor of St. Peter). The "soul" of the Church is the Holy Spirit, and there is only one Spirit. (cf. Eph. 4:4)

Holy. God revealed that marriage is designed to be the union of *one* man and *one* woman. (cf. Gen. 2:24) Jesus Christ identifies himself as the "bridegroom." (Matt. 9:15; 25:1-13) The bride of Jesus the Lamb is the holy and new city of Jerusalem, in whom dwell all God's faithful people. (cf. Rev. 21:2) This city is identified with the Church by St. Paul in two places: first, he says to the Corinthians, "I betrothed you to Christ to present you as a pure bride to her one husband" (2 Cor. 11:2); second, he says to the Ephesians:

> [T]he husband is the head of the wife as Christ is the head of the Church, his body, and is himself its Savior. As the Church is subject to Christ, so let wives also be subject in everything to their husbands. *Husbands, love your wives, as Christ loved the Church* and gave himself up for her, that he might sanctify her, having cleansed her by the washing of water with the word, that he might present the Church to himself in splendor, without spot or wrinkle

> or any such thing, *that she might be holy* and without blemish. ...
> "For this reason a man shall leave his father and mother and be
> joined to his wife, and the two shall become one flesh." This is *a
> great mystery*, and I mean in reference to *Christ and the Church*.
> (Eph. 5:23-32)

Because Christ gave Himself up for the Church, He sanctified her, that is,
He made her holy.

Catholic. The Church is "catholic," that is, *universal*. By His blood,
Christ ransomed men for God "from every tribe and tongue and people
and nation." (Rev. 5:9) The sacrament of Baptism, by which a person
enters the Church, can be received by *anyone*, Jew or Gentile, slave or
free, male or female. (cf. Gal. 3:28) The word "catholic" comes from the
Greek word *katholikos*, which is derived from *kata* ("according to") and
holos ("the whole"). The phrase *"ekklesiai kath olos"* appears in Acts 9:31:
"the *Church throughout all* Judea and Galilee and Samaria had peace and
was built up." The Church is catholic, even though it has a multitude of
liturgical Rites. Not all Catholics are "Roman Catholic" (meaning they
worship according to the Roman Rite), although all Catholics are in
communion with the Church of Rome; some other Catholic Rites are
Byzantine, Ruthenian, Mozarabic, Ambrosian, and Melkite. A Catholic
of *any* Rite can go to a Mass or Divine Liturgy in *any* Catholic Rite and
receive Communion. The fact that St. Paul wrote to so many churches
(all belonging to the *one* Church) to keep them in the true doctrine shows
that he had a universal ("catholic") concern, what he called a "care for all
the churches" (2 Cor. 11:28), to ensure that the *same faith* be held *by all*
who confess belief in Christ.

Apostolic. The Church is founded by Jesus Christ *on* the Apostles.
Jesus chose St. Peter specifically as the "rock" and guarantor of the true
faith. (Matt. 16:18-19; cf. Luke 22:31-32) The Apostles are the "first" in
the Church (1 Cor. 12:28), because they are sent forth (which is what
apostolos means) to spread the Gospel, and because of their work the rest
of the body of the Church is formed. St. Paul speaks of the Church as
the "household of God, built upon *the foundation of the apostles and prophets*,
Christ Jesus himself being the cornerstone." (Eph. 2:19-20) The Roman
Canon (Eucharistic Prayer I) includes a prayer for "all those who, holding
to the truth, hand on the *catholic and apostolic faith*."

There has been a slight change in the translation of this clause of the Creed: we no longer say that we believe *in the Church*, but that we believe *the Church*. We do not believe *in* the Church as we believe *in* God, but we do believe the Church is ordained by God and we believe the Church as the guardian and teacher of the faith. We accept in faith the mysteries revealed by God to His Church, even if we cannot *understand* them. The Roman Catechism explains the difference in terminology in this way:

> [H]ere we make use of a different form of expression, professing to believe *the holy*, not *in the holy* Catholic Church. By this difference of expression we distinguish God, the author of all things, from His works... (*Roman Catechism*, Creed, IX)

The Communion of Saints

Article nine of the Apostles' Creed includes both "the holy catholic Church" and "the communion of saints." The Catechism explains that the "communion of saints" is, in a certain sense, a way of describing what "the holy catholic Church" is. (cf. *Catechism* 946-947)

St. John, in his first letter, wrote that he proclaimed the "word of life ... made manifest ... so that you may have fellowship with us; and our *fellowship is with the Father and with his Son Jesus Christ*." (1 John 1:1-3) This fellowship is the basis of the "communion of saints." There are many layers to this communion, but they all depend upon the unity of the Church ("one") which is brought about and sanctified by the Holy Spirit ("holy"), such that whatever has been bestowed to the Church is held in common by all her members ("catholic"). This was evident especially in the newborn Church: "all who believed *were together* and had *all things in common*; and they sold their possessions and goods and *distributed them to all*, as any had need." (Acts 2:44-45)

This passage from Scripture makes it clear that this communion involved both *things* and *people*. In fact, the Latin expression *sanctorum communionem* means both "the communion of holy *people*" (the saints) and "the communion of holy *things*." [8] (cf. *Catechism* 960-961) What are some of these holy things?

---

[8] In many of the Eastern liturgies of the Church, the acclamation "holy things for holy people" is said before the reception of Communion as a reminder that God's holy people are fed by the holy Body and Blood of His Son. (cf. *Catechism* 948)

Communion of Faith. Since the earliest days, all the members of the Church have "devoted themselves to the apostles' teaching and fellowship, to the breaking of the bread and the prayers." (Acts 2:42) All the members of the Church share a single common faith which is handed on by the Apostles. (cf. *Catechism* 949)

Communion of Sacraments. The sacraments, and especially the Eucharist, are the pre-eminent holy "things" of the Church. People are brought into communion with the Church by means of the sacrament of Baptism. Thus, Baptism is the door to communion, and all who are in the Church benefit from the sacraments, even those they do not personally receive. For example, the sacraments of Holy Orders and Matrimony are called "sacraments at the service of communion," because they serve to build up the Church and sanctify her members: a layperson benefits from the ministry of the Church's deacons, priests, and bishops, and the children from a marriage benefit from the sacrament received by their parents. The sacrament of the Eucharist actually *produces* in the Church's members this communion. (cf. *Catechism* 950)

Communion of Charity. Every vocation and good work among the members of the Church is profitable to all the other members. St. Paul describes the mystical connection of these gifts and works among the members of the Church in his first letter to the Corinthians:

> Now there are varieties of gifts, but the same Spirit; and there are varieties of service, but the same Lord; and there are varieties of working, but it is the same God who inspires them all in every one. To each is given the manifestation of the Spirit *for the common good.* ... For just as the body is one and has many members, and all the members of the body, though many, are one body, so it is with Christ. ... But God has so composed the body, giving the greater honor to the inferior part, that there may be no discord in the body, but *that the members may have the same care for one another.* If one member suffers, *all suffer together;* if one member is honored, *all rejoice together.* (1 Cor. 12:4-26)

Every spiritual gift bestowed on the members of the Church, and every good work performed by her members, serves to build up the Church as a whole. Conversely, the sin of one member affects other members and harms the communion. (cf. *Catechism* 951-953)

Communion of People. The communion of saints, as holy people, is distributed among three groups: the Church Militant (pilgrims here on earth), the Church Suffering (those being purified in Purgatory), and the Church Triumphant (those enjoying eternal bliss in the glory of Heaven). Death does not separate us from Christ (cf. Rom. 8:38-39), so we remain in communion with those who have died in Christ, and we benefit from their intercession. Those who have endured the trials of this life and are in Heaven are witnesses of our struggles on earth, as the letter to the Hebrews states: "we are surrounded by so great a cloud of witnesses" (Heb. 12:1) comprised of those who have gone before us in faith. These three groups are in communion with each other through Christ: we can assist the souls in Purgatory by our prayers and good deeds, and the saints in Heaven can assist us by their intercession. (cf. *Catechism* 954-959)

One Baptism for the Forgiveness of Sins

The Apostles' Creed professes faith in the forgiveness of sins, that sins can be and *are* forgiven. The Nicene Creed says that there is *one baptism* for this forgiveness. There are two important elements in this clause: there is only *one baptism* and it *bestows forgiveness.*

One Baptism. Jesus at His Ascension charged the Church with the mission to "make disciples of all nations, *baptizing them* in the name of the Father and of the Son and of the Holy Spirit, *teaching them* to observe all that I have commanded you." (Matt. 28:19-20) Disciples of Christ are made through Baptism and catechesis in the faith. The Church knows, as St. Paul taught, that there is only *one* Baptism. (cf. Eph. 4:5) So long as a man is baptized with the Trinitarian formula in water, he is validly baptized into Christ's Church (although perhaps not in full communion with it); this is why a man brought up in, for example, a Baptist or Presbyterian community does not need to be re-baptized if he seeks full communion with the Catholic Church, provided he *has* been baptized validly. Baptism places an indelible mark on our soul that can never be removed: there is only one Baptism and we may be baptized only once.

Forgiveness of Sins. Among the various Protestant communities, there are many differing theologies on just what Baptism is. Some call it an "ordinance" (a command) rather than a "sacrament." Some do not believe that infants can be validly baptized. Some do not believe it is necessary to be baptized. Some do not believe it saves a person or brings him forgiveness of his sins. What the Catholic Church teaches is that Baptism is a sacrament[9] ordinarily necessary for salvation (cf. John 3:3-5) which forgives the baptized of all sin (original and actual) and removes all punishment due to that sin. (cf. Acts 2:38; 22:16; *Catechism* 978, 1999) Infants can and *should* be baptized as soon as is practical, although they have committed no personal sin, because they are conceived with the inherited original sin of Adam. Baptism is to the new covenant what circumcision was to the old covenant: the sign by which a person enters the covenant. Baptism saves us (cf. 1 Pet. 3:20-21), although it does not guarantee our salvation in and of itself. Baptism remits whatever actual sins we have committed *before* we receive it, but not those committed *after* we receive it; Christ gave His Church the sacrament of Confession for the purpose of reconciling those who sin after baptism.

The Resurrection

The simplest explanation of the resurrection is that our physical bodies will be restored and reunited with our souls. We do not believe that we will simply be disembodied (or worse yet, "freed") spirits floating around Heaven for eternity (although the souls of the saints are in Heaven until the time of the resurrection), but that our souls and bodies will be united once more.[10] Not only that, but our bodies will be "spiritual" bodies rather than "natural" bodies.

What is a "spiritual" body? It is a *glorified* body, like Jesus had at His Transfiguration (cf. Matt. 17:1-8) and after His Resurrection. We will still be *ourselves* and retain our *substance*, although we may not appear *exactly* the same as we do now, as Jesus was not immediately recognized in His glorified body. (cf. Luke 24:16; John 20:14-15) We will not be pure spirit (like the Father or the Holy Spirit), but we will have flesh and bones as does Jesus. (cf. Luke 24:39) But at the same time, our bodies will be in a new condition, endowed with supernatural qualities: for example, Jesus

---

[9] A sacrament is an outward (visible) sign, instituted by Christ, which bestows grace.

[10] There are at least two human bodies in Heaven: Jesus and the Blessed Virgin Mary, who was assumed body and soul into Heaven at the end of her earthly life. (cf. *Catechism* 974) In Jesus and His mother there is represented the fullness of redeemed humanity, Jesus as the new Adam and the Blessed Virgin Mary as the new Eve. There *might* be more humans with bodies in Heaven, such as Moses, Elijah, and Enoch.

disappeared from sight (cf. Luke 24:31) and could pass through locked doors. (cf. John 20:19, 26) St. Paul wrote to the Corinthians concerning the manner of body we will have in the resurrection:

> But some one will ask, "How are the dead raised? With what kind of body do they come?" ... *What is sown is perishable, what is raised is imperishable.* It is sown in dishonor, it is raised in glory. It is sown in weakness, it is raised in power. *It is sown a physical body, it is raised a spiritual body.* ... Behold! I tell you a mystery. We shall not all sleep, but we shall all be changed, in a moment, in the twinkling of an eye, at the last trumpet. For the trumpet will sound, and the dead will be raised imperishable, and we shall be changed. For *this perishable nature must put on the imperishable*, and *this mortal nature must put on immortality.* (1 Cor. 15:35-53)

No matter what happens to our bodies at or after death, whether we are cremated or decay – or, as some early Christians worried, eaten by wild beasts who are then eaten by other people! – our bodies will be restored to completion in the resurrection. There is some speculation as to whether the wounds that martyrs received for Christ's sake will remain perceptible in some way, just as Jesus, in His glorified body, retained the holes in His hands, feet, and side. (cf. Luke 24:39; John 20:27; Rev. 5:6) We can be sure, though, that our glorified bodies will be dignified and perfected so as to render perfect glory to God by their very nature. [11]

Amen!

With that, the Creed ends with a resounding *Amen!* This is the faith of the Church, the faith which leads us to everlasting life, so we should be joyful to hold it... but also to share it with others so that they too might know the surpassing grace, mercy, and love of God in Jesus Christ.

I can imagine you wondering how *all that* is a *prayer*. It seems more like an elementary school essay, "What I Believed Last Summer." How can a statement of beliefs be a prayer to God? The answer lies in the relation between the Creed and the *Shema*. A Jew prays the *Shema* to glorify God,

---

[11] St. Paul wrote that the resurrection of the dead is utterly foundational to our faith: "if there is no resurrection of the dead, then Christ has not been raised; if Christ has not been raised, then our preaching is in vain and your faith is in vain ... and you are still in your sins. ... If for this life only we have hoped in Christ, we are of all men most to be pitied." (1 Cor. 15:13-19)

but also to remind himself of who he is and to form his life more in accordance with the knowledge he has of God. The same is true of the Creed. It is a sort of "mission statement," but the mission is that of the Church. In the Creed, we profess our beliefs and pray that we would truly believe what the Church proposes for our belief so that we might better carry out the Church's mission. [12]

As you say (or sing) the Creed, think of the martyrs of the faith who died for professing what you can say without fear: you believe in one God, the Father, and in one Lord Jesus Christ, His only-begotten Son, and in the Holy Spirit, the Lord, the giver of life, and the one Church which He established. This is the faith of the Church, the faith which comes to us from the Apostles.

After the Creed comes the Prayer of the Faithful, when we pray for the Church, the world, the greatest and the least, the living and the dead. The Prayer of the Faithful is an example of our faith, as expressed in the Creed, being put into action.

Questions for Reflection

1) **Interpret:** The first time that the word "believe" appears in the Bible is in Genesis 15:5-6, describing Abram's response to God's promise to give him descendents as numerous as the stars. Why is belief (*faith* and *trust*) necessary in our relationship with God?

2) **Interpret:** The definition of "faith" is given in Hebrews 11:1-6. How are the things we profess in the Creed "things hoped for, … things not seen"?

3) **Interpret:** Jesus asked His disciples who the people thought the Son of Man was. After they gave Him a list of guesses, He asked them who *they* thought the Son of Man was, and Simon answered, "You are the Christ, the Son of the living God." Jesus told Simon that it was not flesh and blood which revealed this to him, but God the Father. (cf. Matt. 16:13-17) Is the Creed simply our guess of Who God is and what His Church is, or is it something more?

---

[12] The *Catechism* (paragraphs 185-1065) and its *Compendium* (questions 33-217) are indispensible resources for understanding what the Church teaches through the Creeds.

4) **Explain:** Why do we stand during the Profession of Faith?

5) **Explain:** Creeds were often composed to correct a particular misunderstanding of the Church's faith. Which of the Church's beliefs are not mentioned in these Creeds that you would have expected to see?

6) **Relate:** C.S. Lewis wondered why the Apostles' Creed mentions the forgiveness of sin. Which of the propositions seems the most obvious to you? Have you ever wondered *why* we profess it?

7) **Relate:** "I believe; help my unbelief!" (Mark 9:24) These are the words of a father who approached Jesus to ask Him to heal his possessed son. Which proposition in the Creeds is the easiest for you to accept? Which is the hardest?

8) **Relate:** How does the Creed define (and challenge) you as a Catholic? What does it affirm in you, and what more does it call you to?

"Hear, O hear me, God of my father, God of the inheritance of Israel,
Lord of heaven and earth, Creator of the waters,
King of all your creation, hear my prayer!"
(Judith 9:12)

Pray at all times in the Spirit, with all prayer and supplication.
To that end keep alert with all perseverance,
making supplication for all the saints.
(Ephesians 6:18)

8

Prayer of the Faithful

FOR THE PAST several centuries (up until the 1960s), the Roman Rite of the Mass did not include what we call the "Prayer of the Faithful," the "Universal Prayer," or the "General Intercessions." These prayers were only offered during the Good Friday liturgy commemorating the Passion and death of our Lord. This seems contrary to one of the earliest records of liturgical practice in Rome that we have, from the "Apology" of St. Justin Martyr, who wrote that after the Scriptures were read and a sermon was given, "we all rise together and pray" (*Apology* I, 67), after which the bread and wine for the Eucharist were brought forward. This rising and praying together is understood to be referring to what we call today the "Prayer of the Faithful."

It has been suggested that the Roman Canon (Eucharistic Prayer I), which was the only Eucharistic Prayer for the Roman Rite for around 1500 years, includes petitions similar to those which would be offered in the Prayer of the Faithful, so it took the place of a separate liturgical act; in favor of this theory, it is pointed out that the only day on which General Intercessions were offered was the *one* day on which the Roman Canon was not prayed, Good Friday, because there is no Mass celebrated on that day. One of the liturgical changes mandated in the Constitution on the Sacred Liturgy was the restoration of these prayers:

> [T]here is to be restored, after the Gospel and the homily, "the common prayer" or "the prayer of the faithful." By this prayer, in which the people are to take part, intercession will be made for holy Church, for the civil authorities, for those oppressed by various needs, for all mankind, and for the salvation of the entire world. (CSL 53)

This tradition of praying for the Church, for civil leaders, for the oppressed, for the good of all men, and especially for their salvation, comes to us from St. Paul, who exhorted the young Bishop St. Timothy:

> I urge that supplications, prayers, intercessions, and thanksgivings be made for *all men*, for *kings* and *all who are in high positions*, that we may lead a quiet and peaceable life, godly and respectful in every way. This is good, and it is acceptable in the sight of *God our Savior, who desires all men to be saved* and to come to the knowledge of the truth. For there is one God, and *there is one mediator* between God and men, the man Christ Jesus. (1 Tim. 2:1-4)

To offer intercessions is to intercede for another person; to *intercede* means "to go" (*cedere*) "between" (*inter-*). In other words, an intercessor is a mediator. But if "there is one mediator" between God and men, and that is Jesus Christ, how can *we* be mediators? How can we intercede for another, if we are not the Son of God? To answer that question, we should first consider the unbaptized who are seeking entrance into the Church (usually through the Rite of Christian Initiation of Adults).

These unbaptized men and women are called *catechumens*, from the Greek word meaning "one being instructed." (The same root gives us the words "catechesis" and "catechism.") If there are any catechumens present at Mass, they are customarily dismissed after the homily and before the Creed, because they have not yet assented to the Creed as they will at their baptism. If they enter the Church at the Easter Vigil, the Rite of Baptism takes place after the homily, which means that after they receive Baptism and Confirmation, the very next liturgical rite they will encounter is the Prayer of the Faithful, in which, as St. Paul describes, we offer "supplications, prayers, *intercessions*, and thanksgivings."

When the newly baptized finally get to participate in the General Intercessions, they will "for the first time as members of the faithful exercise their priesthood" (*Paschale Solemnitatis* 91) by "offer[ing] prayers to God for the salvation of all." (GIRM 69) Through baptism into Christ's body, they become sharers (as we are) in His priesthood. The primary duty of a priest is to intercede for his people; Christ, our High Priest, "holds his priesthood permanently" and "is able for all time to save those who draw near to God through him, since *he always lives to make intercession for them*." (Heb. 7:24-25) We exercise the priesthood of Christ by interceding for others, although in a different manner from a ministerial (ordained) priest.

St. Thomas Aquinas explained that only Christ, the High priest, is the true priest; all other priests are only His ministers. (cf. *Catechism* 1545) It is in this way that we can intercede for the world, by being ministers of the mediator between God and man. By our baptism, we are enabled to be *co*-mediators: mediators *with* Christ, but not in place of Him (since we offer our prayers through Him) nor equal to Him (because He is both man *and* God). This co-working with Christ is only possible through our baptism, in which we "put on Christ" (Gal. 3:27) so that it is no longer ourselves who live, but Christ Who lives in us. (cf. Gal 2:20)

The *General Instruction of the Roman Missal* directs that the intentions should follow this order:

> a. For the needs of the Church; b. For public authorities and the salvation of the whole world; c. For those burdened by any kind of difficulty; d. For the local community. (GIRM 70)

The prayers usually include mention of those in the local community who are sick or have died. There is also usually a time for us to make our own silent petitions in our hearts. While there is no standardized form for the intentions nor the response of the people, the Missal does provide example formulas. If the form of the Prayer of the Faithful requires the people to make a response after each intention, the Missal suggests one of the following:

Kýrie, eléison. *or:* **Dómine, miserére.**

Lord, have mercy. *Matt. 20:30*

Or:

Præsta, omnípotens Deus.

Grant it (*or:* this), Almighty God. *Jdth. 13:20; Phlm. 1:22*

Or:

Christe, audi nos. *or:* **Exáudi, Christe.**

Christ, hear us.   *Jdth. 9:4; Mic. 7:7; Jer. 29:12*
or: Lord, hear our prayer.   *Jdth. 9:12*

The most common response in the English-speaking world is probably "Lord, hear our prayer." It might seem odd to you to respond with "Lord, have mercy" to a prayer of intercession, but this is actually an ancient and venerable tradition found especially in the Eastern Churches, whose liturgies include fixed sets of intercessions with this response. The use of "grant this" or "grant it" is common in the prayers which the priest offers: "Grant this through Christ our Lord."

These prayers are not an "intermission" or "break" in between the Liturgy of the Word and the Liturgy of the Eucharist. Rather, they are a confident expression of our trust in God to hear and answer our prayers. In offering these intentions, we imitate our ancestors in faith, and we call upon God to come to the aid of His people.

As each intercession is read, listen closely. Your duty is not simply to say "Lord, hear our prayer" and get on with your life. These petitions which are offered to God are not the sole responsibility of the person reading them in the midst of the assembly, they are *your* responsibility too. Make it a point to take at least *one* of them deep into your heart. Throughout the week, make an effort to pray daily for that need.

To that end, it would be a great help for pastors to consider making these intercessions available to parishioners so that the Prayer of the Faithful in the *church* might also become the Prayer of the Faithful in the *domestic* church, the home. Consider preceding the prayer of blessing for your dinner with one of these petitions and a moment of private, silent prayer for that intention. If participation in the liturgy of the Church is "the primary and indispensable source from which the faithful are to derive the true Christian spirit" as the Constitution on the Sacred Liturgy says it is, then drawing from that source when *outside* the liturgy can only serve to fill your daily life more deeply with that true Christian spirit.

And now, having offered our petitions to God, we next prepare to offer a living sacrifice – not just of ourselves, but of the Body and Blood of Jesus Christ. The next liturgical action, then, is the preparation and offering of the bread and wine.

Questions for Reflection

1) **Interpret:** Those who were devout in their faith were often called upon as intercessors, for example Abraham (cf. Gen. 20:7), Job (cf. Job 42:8), and Judith (cf. Jdth. 8:31). Where in the New Testament do we see interceding for friends *and* enemies as an important duty of a faithful follower of Christ?

2) **Interpret:** The intentions of the Prayer of the Faithful are like a litany, where a petition or statement is made by one person and the rest of the people respond with an acclamation used over and over again. Pray Psalm 136. While this litany-psalm concentrates on thanksgiving rather than on petition, how does it resemble the Prayer of the Faithful?

3) **Explain:** The repeated phrase in Psalm 136 can be translated as "his *love* endures forever" (NAB) or as "his *mercy* endures for ever" (RSV, 2nd Catholic Edition). Why is "Lord, have mercy" a logical response to the petitions of the Prayer of the Faithful, as it is used in the Eastern Rites?

4) **Relate:** The mission of the Church is the salvation of souls. How does the Prayer of the Faithful serve this mission?

5) **Relate:** Is *prayer* the only way the Church fulfills this mission? What should the Prayer of the Faithful motivate us to do?

With a freewill offering I will sacrifice to you;
I will give thanks to your name, O LORD, for it is good.
(Psalm 54:6)

By the mercies of God, present your bodies as a living sacrifice,
holy and acceptable to God, which is your spiritual worship.
(Romans 12:1)

9

Offertory Prayers

THE LITURGY OF THE Eucharist is composed of three parts: first is the *Offertory*, during which the bread and wine are brought to the altar and prepared and offered to God; second is the *Eucharistic Prayer*, during which the bread and wine are consecrated, becoming the Eucharist, which is then offered to God; and third is the *Communion Rite*, during which the sacrifice is consumed by the priest, who then offers it to us as well, ending with the post-Communion prayer.

There is a great exchange which takes place during this part of the Mass. We acknowledge that God has given us bread and wine, which we in turn offer back to Him. God accepts our offering and, by the power of the Holy Spirit acting through the priest, gives us back the Eucharist. The priest then offers the Eucharist immediately back to the Father in the second half of the Eucharistic Prayer. God is pleased by this most perfect sacrifice and in His great mercy He permits us to receive His Son in Holy Communion.

The Offertory prayers are said during the preparation of the bread and wine. There are six prayers said by the priest, but we will look at the three to which we respond. These are the "Blessed are you, Lord..." prayers, one said over the bread and the other over the chalice, and the prayer said after the priest has washed his hands and invites us with the words "Pray, brethren…" to pray for the acceptance of the bread and wine (and in turn, the Eucharist) as well as our own personal offerings.

Offertory Procession

An external act which represents an internal reality is empty unless that internal reality is truly present. Imagine a man giving his wife a bouquet of roses, a gesture generally recognized as a display of love, without actually caring about her at all. The roses are real, the wife's reaction is real, but there is something missing: the intention. This analogy can be applied to the Offertory Procession, when bread and wine are brought to the priest. This external act, often carried out by members of the congregation,[1] is not a mere functional procedure; it is representative of so much more.

In the ancient Church, the bread and wine would often be personally supplied by members of the faithful. Nowadays, the bread and wine are usually purchased by with parish funds (which ultimately come from the faithful), so they still represent *our* offering, *our* presentation to the Lord. This presentation is an external manifestation of the internal self-offering which we are called to make during the Mass: the bread and wine are not just the necessary matter for celebrating the Eucharist, they also represent *all* that we have to offer to God. Pope John Paul II, in his 1980 letter to Bishops on the Eucharist, explained this rite's significance:

> Although all those who participate in the Eucharist do not confect the sacrifice as [the priest] does, they offer with him, by virtue of the common priesthood, *their own spiritual sacrifices represented by the bread and wine* from the moment of their presentation at the altar. … The bread and wine become in a sense *a symbol of all that the eucharistic assembly brings*, on its own part, as an offering to God and offers spiritually. (*Dominicae Cenae* 9)

Just as the bread and wine are presented to the priest who offers them to God, we offer *ourselves* to God as a spiritual sacrifice by virtue of our baptismal priesthood. Archbishop Fulton J. Sheen, in his 1936 missal companion *Calvary and the Mass*, wrote about this self-offering:

---

[1] "It is praiseworthy for the bread and wine to be presented by the faithful." (GIRM 73)

We are therefore present at each and every Mass under the appearance of bread and wine, which stand as symbols of *our* body and blood. We are not passive spectators as we might be watching a spectacle in a theater, but *we are co-offering* our Mass with Christ. [We] offer ourselves in union with Him, as a clean oblation to the heavenly Father. (*The Offertory*)

The only sacrifice that is truly acceptable to God the Father is the Eucharist, which is the very Body, Blood, Soul, and Divinity of His Son, our Lord Jesus Christ. But God looks on what we offer with fatherly affection. The bread and wine presented to Him by the priest is deemed acceptable as the means by which He will give us the Eucharist; the bread and wine are gifts from God to begin with. Because the bread and wine represent our spiritual sacrifices, these too are regarded with a similar love. God knows what He will make of the bread and wine, and He knows what He will make of our meager sacrifices.

Once the bread and wine have been placed on the altar, the priest prepares them for the Eucharistic Prayer and prays over them.

"Blessed be God forever."

The prayers over the bread and over the chalice are not always said aloud by the priest. When the Offertory chant or a hymn is being sung, the priest prays them quietly (*not* silently, cf. GIRM 33) and the congregation does not make a response; if there is no singing, the priest *may* choose to say them quietly or aloud. If he says them aloud, the congregation makes the following response for both prayers:

Benedíctus Deus in sǽcula.

Blessed be God forever. *1 Chr. 16:36; Ps. 41:13; Dan. 2:20; Rom. 9:5*

This response is our affirmation of the words at the beginning of the prayers said by the priest: "Blessed are you, Lord, ..." The prayers of the priest identify God as the origin of the bread and the wine which we offer back to Him.

In our response, we affirm an eternal truth: God is blessed over all of His creation. But we do not mention ourselves or anything else in all of God's creation in the response. We do not say "*We* bless you forever, God," or "Blessed be God forever, Who gives *us* all these gifts." Instead, we forget ourselves and humbly confess the blessedness which is God's in and of Himself.

The bread and wine are blessed by these prayers; they are set aside for the Eucharistic Prayer, when they will become the Body and Blood of Christ. But in that brief time between the Offertory and Consecration, the bread and wine are **sacramentals** because of the prayer of the priest over them. A sacramental, such as the bread or wine to be used in the Eucharistic Prayer, or a paten or chalice, is dedicated for a particular use when blessed. This is not the same as the change that takes place in a sacrament (such as the Eucharist), where bread and wine change *ontologically* (that is, in their *substance*). A sacrament involves a change of being, whereas a sacramental involves a change of purpose.

By uniting our spiritual sacrifices to the bread and wine in the Offertory, we "appropriate" those sacramentals, much in the same way we "appropriate" holy water (another sacramental) by being blessed with it, or we "appropriate" a blessing over a meal by praying it. We join our *spiritual* sacrifices to the bread and wine (which represent, *physically*, those very sacrifices), imbuing them with a greater spiritual significance for each of us and for the Church as a whole.

"May the Lord accept..."

After the priest has prayed over the bread and wine and washed his hands, the congregation stands and the priest invites the faithful to pray (the *Orate fratres*, "Pray brethren") that the sacrifice being offered will be accepted by God. We respond:

**Suscípiat Dóminus sacrifícium de mánibus tuis
ad laudem et glóriam nóminis sui,
ad utilitátem quoque nostram totiúsque Ecclésiæ suæ sanctæ.**

May the Lord accept the sacrifice at your hands,	*1 Cor. 11:24-25; 1 Pet. 2:5*
for the praise and glory of his name,	*1 Chr. 16:29; Joel 2:26*
for our good	*Matt. 26:27; Mark 14:24; Luke 22:19-20*
» and the good of all his holy Church.	*Eph. 4:12; 5:25-30*

The priest speaks of "my sacrifice and yours" (*meum ac vestrum sacrifícium*). In the old translation this was rendered as "*our* sacrifice," but the Latin distinguishes between what the priest brings to the sacrifice and what we bring to it. The priest offers the bread and wine (and the Eucharist); we participate in the offering by the priest and join to it *our very selves.*

The bread and wine are changed into the Real Presence of Jesus Christ at the consecration of the Eucharistic Prayer, but this presence is hidden under what the Church calls a "sacramental veil," the remaining appearance of bread and wine. When we see Christ in Heaven, there will be no veil. In much the same way, we pray that we may be changed to be more like Christ ("configured" to Christ, in the language of the Church) by receiving Holy Communion. This configuration to Christ is imperfect while we are on earth, but it will be perfected when our resurrected and glorified bodies enter Heaven.

Just as the bread and wine will be transubstantiated into Christ, what they *represent* – ourselves, the Church, the Body of Christ – is, in a sense, transubstantiated as well. By identifying ourselves with the bread and wine, as Archbishop Sheen wrote, we are anticipating the change which will occur in us at the end of time while conforming our lives to the change taking place now.

Because of what the bread and wine will become (once consecrated), the union of our spiritual sacrifices to the bread and wine during the Offertory is a sign of our participation in Christ and His sacrifice. The bread and wine already have a *physical* likeness to Christ's sacrifice, because they are the same elements He used, and the same elements that were offered centuries before Him by Melchizedek. (cf. Gen. 14:18) When we join our spiritual sacrifices to them in the Offertory, each of us gives them a *spiritual* likeness to Christ's sacrifice. Finally, in the Eucharistic Prayer, this likeness is perfected as they receive a *substantial* likeness to Christ's sacrifice.

The bread and wine (and afterwards, the Eucharist) and ourselves are united as *one* at the hands of the priest: he offers them physically as we offer them spiritually. The bread and wine which the priest holds during the words of consecration represent us, since they represent the fruits of our labor. Then, as the priest offers the Eucharist to God, we join our very lives – all of our worries, cares, sufferings, and prayers – to Christ in the Eucharist. It is only by joining ourselves to Christ, the perfect sacrifice, that the contribution of our living, spiritual sacrifice can be truly acceptable to the Father. (cf. Rom. 12:1; 1 Pet. 2:5)[2]

Archbishop Charles Chaput, O.F.M. Cap., of Denver, wrote about the Offertory prayers in a weekly column in December 2002: "This part of the Mass is another invitation for us to offer our lives in a sacrifice of praise to God. Here the common priesthood actively engages in the sacrifice taking place." This common or baptismal priesthood is part of our identity in Christ. In a sermon from the 5th century, St. Peter Chrysologus, the Bishop of Ravenna (in northern Italy) spoke to his flock about St. Paul's words in Romans 12:1.

> Listen now to what the Apostle urges us to do: "I appeal to you," he says, "to present your bodies as a living sacrifice." By this exhortation of his, Paul has raised all men to *priestly status*.
>
> How marvelous is the priesthood of the Christian, for he is both the victim that is offered on his own behalf, and the priest who makes the offering. He does not need to go beyond himself to seek what he is to immolate to God: with himself and in himself he brings the sacrifice he is to offer God for himself.

In a Christian's self-offering to God, he is following the pattern of Christ Who is both priest and victim. Because Christ is both priest and victim, our share in His priesthood (exercised in intercessory prayer, as well as in this offering of ourselves as living sacrifices of praise) must also include a share in His victimhood. This does not mean that we should expect to undergo a persecution and death as grievous as His, but we should unite the suffering we encounter in our lives to the suffering that Christ endured for our sake. The words of St. Paul to the Colossians are particularly meaningful in this regard: "Now I rejoice in my sufferings for your sake, and in my flesh I complete what is lacking in Christ's afflictions for the sake of his body, that is, the Church." (Col. 1:24) St. Paul is not saying that Christ's sufferings were imperfect or incomplete, but that our participation in Christ's sufferings has yet to be fulfilled; in St. Paul's suffering for the sake of the Church, he is completing his participation in Christ's life, which he began in his baptism.

Heed the Lord's words which call us to a life of self-offering:

---

[2] See the Appendix for excerpts from several Church documents (including *Mediator Dei* of Pope Pius XII) which provide a liturgical spirituality through which we learn to join ourselves to Christ.

"Unless a grain of wheat falls into the earth and dies, it remains alone; but *if it dies, it bears much fruit.* He who loves his life loses it, and he who hates his life in this world will keep it for eternal life. If any one serves me, he must follow me." (John 12:24-26)

Jesus is the true Bread from Heaven, the very "grain" of Heaven. The model He gave us is one of voluntary sacrifice for the good of others. That concern for the good of others is the motivation behind the words we say.

We pray that the Lord will accept the sacrifice for three goods: for the increase of praise and glory to His own holy name, for our good (we who are making this offering), and for the good of *all* His holy Church; the old translation omitted the word "holy," but this word has been restored in the new translation. The praise and glory of God and His name is one of the four ends for which Mass is celebrated, and it is particularly by the offering of the Eucharist that He is perfectly glorified. The priest offering the sacrifice, and we who unite ourselves to it and offer it through his hands, benefit by means of that union with the Lord and especially by the graces received in Holy Communion.

As for the good of all the Church, a person need not be present at Mass to receive graces from it. Some Masses are offered particularly for some person or group of people. In addition, remember that the Church is not just made up of those living on earth, but includes those who are undergoing purification in Purgatory. The sacrifice of the Mass is offered for *their* benefit as well as our own, and each Eucharistic Prayer includes a prayer for the dead. Finally, when the Mass commemorates saints or angels, they are sure to rejoice in God by Whose grace they merited the honor we give them. In this way, not only is the Mass offered for the good of the whole Church, but we again carry out our priestly duty of interceding by offering the Mass for the good of others.

The Offertory is a time of preparation. Before Mass began, we started to prepare ourselves by blessing ourselves with holy water and the Sign of the Cross. As Mass began, we asked God for His mercy and forgiveness. Throughout the Liturgy of the Word, we were reminded of the covenant

God has formed with us through His Son; we were instructed in the homily as to how to live according to that covenant.

St. Peter Chrysologus ended his sermon with a challenge to live as self-sacrificing priests. First, he spoke of the preparation necessary:

> Each of us is called to be both a sacrifice to God and his priest. Do not forfeit what divine authority confers on you. Put on the garment of holiness, gird yourself with the belt of chastity. Let Christ be your helmet, let the cross on your forehead be your unfailing protection. Your breastplate should be the knowledge of God that he himself has given you. Keep burning continually the sweet smelling incense of prayer. Take up the sword of the Spirit. Let your heart be an altar.

Once you are prepared, spiritually clothed in priestly attire and standing at the altar of your heart, ready to serve the Lord, then:

> with full confidence in God, present your body for sacrifice. God desires not death, but faith; God thirsts not for blood, but for self-surrender; God is appeased not by slaughter, but by the offering of your free will.

This is the spiritual attitude we must strive to adopt in our daily lives, but especially during the Mass.

The last part of the Offertory is the Prayer over the Offerings which the priest prays aloud; we respond "Amen." Then, with the preparation of the bread and wine (and of ourselves) completed, the priest begins the Eucharistic Prayer in which the miracle of the Mass takes place.

Questions for Reflection

1) **Interpret:** The Passover lambs had to be perfect and without blemish. Why does the Church require pure wheat bread and grape wine, with no additions or substitutions, for the Eucharist?

2) **Interpret:** In Psalm 51:16-19, David writes of the worthlessness of empty sacrifices. Why does the Mass begin with a Penitential Act before the offering of the Eucharist?

3) **Explain:** How are bread and wine symbols of our lives? How are they appropriate signs of the Body and Blood of Christ?

4) **Relate:** St. Ignatius, Bishop of Antioch in the late 1st century and martyr, wrote in a letter to the Church in Rome, "I am the wheat of God, and let me be ground by the teeth of the wild beasts, that

I may be found the pure bread of Christ." How is the Eucharist connected with martyrdom? What is the fruit of such a sacrifice?

5) **Relate:** If your heart is your spiritual altar, as described by St. Peter Chrysologus in his sermon, consider the significance of the words of the priest in the Preface which follows the Offertory: "Lift up your hearts." What are you placing on the altar of your heart, and what does it mean to bring that altar and its offering into the presence of the Lord?

6) **Relate:** How can your daily life be a living sacrifice?

"From the rising of the sun to its setting my name is great among the nations, and in every place incense is offered to my name, and a pure offering; for my name is great among the nations, says the LORD of hosts."
(Malachi 1:11)

I received from the Lord what I also delivered to you, that the Lord Jesus on the night when he was betrayed took bread, and when he had given thanks, he broke it... In the same way also the chalice, after supper...
(1 Corinthians 11:23-25)

10

Eucharistic Prayer

THE VARIOUS EXCHANGES which take place during the Mass culminate in the Liturgy of the Eucharist, when bread and wine are offered to God, Who returns them to us as the Eucharist. This great gift is offered by the priest back to God, Who accepts it and yet gives it back to us as the marriage banquet and covenant meal which signifies and forms our communion with Him and His Church. This ineffable change takes place during the Eucharistic Prayer, the chief prayer of the Mass.

The Eucharistic Prayer is said by the priest alone, but remember that the sacrifice he is consecrating and offering is not just *his*, but *ours* as well. It is not only bread and wine that are present on the altar, but our very lives. In this chapter and the next, a sermon by St. Augustine[1] addressed to the newly initiated will serve as our guide and companion, helping us to recognize what is taking place in the prayers said by the priest and by us, and what is happening on the altar and when we come to receive Communion.

---

[1] Bishop of Hippo (in Algeria, Africa), Church Father, and Doctor of the Church. (A.D. 354-430) The sermon quoted from is no. 272, from Pentecost, A.D. 408, in the author's translation.

Preface Dialogue

What precedes the Eucharistic Prayer is called the Preface, which begins with a short dialogue between the priest and the faithful. This dialogue is truly ancient, found in virtually every early liturgy. First, the priest greets us with "The Lord be with you," and we respond with "And with your spirit." Then the priest says "Lift up your hearts," and we say:

Habémus ad Dóminum.

We lift them up to the Lord. *Lam. 3:41*

First the priest and the congregation pray for the *Lord* to be with *one another*, then we pray that *we* might be with the *Lord*. This situates us and the liturgy firmly in the presence of the heavenly host.

The Latin is more succinct than the English: the priest says "*Sursum corda*," which, according to the translation of Rev. John Zuhlsdorf, can be read as an enthusiastic "Hearts up!" or "Raise your hearts on high!" Our response is literally, "We have [them] present to the Lord." The Latin word *cor* ("heart") means more than just the literal heart; it can also mean "mind, soul, spirit;" in other words, it means the core of the person. It is not just our hearts that we present to God: the priest is calling us to put our whole being in the presence of the Lord.

These words come from the Lamentations of the prophet Jeremiah:

> Let us test and examine our ways, and return to the LORD! Let us lift up our hearts and hands to God in heaven. (Lam. 3:40-41)

Not only does he tell us to lift up our hearts (and souls and minds) and hands (our strength) to God – which requires us to love Him with all we have and all we are (cf. Luke 10:27) – but he reminds us to examine our lives and return to the Lord. He calls us to repentance and self-offering. At the close of many of his sermons, St. Augustine would say "*Conversi ad Dominum*," that is, "Let us turn to the Lord." These words, reminiscent of the words of the prophet Jeremiah, served as a preparation for the lifting up of our hearts and minds to the Lord.

In the Divine Liturgy of St. John Chrysostom, used in some of the Eastern Rites of the Church, this call to lift our hearts is preceded by the "Cherubic Hymn" sung by the people:

> Let us, who mystically represent the Cherubim, and sing the thrice-holy hymn to the life-creating Trinity, *now lay aside all earthly*

cares that we may welcome the King of all, invisibly escorted by angelic hosts. Alleluia, alleluia, alleluia.

That is what "lift up your hearts" is about, laying aside all earthly cares and recognizing *Who* is about to be present, *Who* is about to be in your midst.

The dialogue concludes with the priest saying, "Let us give thanks to the Lord our God." We respond:

Dignum et iustum est.

» It is right and just.   *Ps. 54:6; 92:1; 147:1*

The Greek word for "let us give thanks" is *eucharistisomen*, from which we get the word "Eucharist" which means "thanksgiving." The priest is essentially inviting us to enter into the Eucharistic part of the liturgy, as if he were saying, "Let us 'do' the Eucharist." Our response is short and to the point: it is *right* and *just* to offer the Eucharist to the Lord.

Why is offering the Eucharist "right"? Simply put, because Christ did it and He told His Apostles to continue doing it in His memory: *"Do this* in remembrance of me." (1 Cor. 11:24-25) The concept of *memorial* here is more complex than just remembering something or someone, as with a holiday like Memorial Day. This memorial is more like a Civil War re-enactment, except that the fate of the United States would truly be at stake; it is more like that of the Passover, which made the liberation from Egypt present to every Jewish generation. But these are surpassed by the memorial of the Eucharist by which "the work of our redemption is accomplished." (CSL 2) The same sacrifice which Christ presented in a bloody manner on Calvary is made present to us in an unbloody manner on every Catholic altar in the world, and *we* are made present to *it*.

Why is offering the Eucharist "just"? The sacrifice of the Eucharist is offered for our sins, the very reason that Christ offered himself on the cross. One synonym for "just" is "righteous," which should remind us of Christ's words just before His baptism: St. John the Baptist asked the Lord, "I need to be baptized by you, and do you come to me?" to which Jesus responded, "Let it be so now; for thus it is fitting for us *to fulfill all righteousness*." (Matt. 3:14-15) How did it come to pass that an unworthy sinner offers and holds in his hands the same sacrifice that the Son of God offered Himself? Another synonym for "just" is "lawful," but this is not the "law" that St. Paul described as being unable to justify; this is the *new* law, the Law of Christ. (cf. Gal. 2:16; 6:2) It is lawful and proper to continue offering the sacrifice of the Eucharist, because it is offered for our justification and sanctification.

These words – "We lift them up to the Lord" and "It is right and just" – are not just lip service to tradition, old words that we say because they were said nearly two thousand years ago. These words are prayers that challenge us to sacrifice and to *like it*. They challenge us to offer ourselves to God and hold nothing back, and in doing so, to confess that God deserves nothing less than our best, nothing less than our very lives. These words should instill in us the desire to unite ourselves to that perfect sacrifice of His Son, to become, like St. Ignatius, "the wheat of God … the pure bread of Christ."

Preface

With this mindset, the priest now prays the Preface, which introduces the Eucharistic Prayer in the context of the current liturgical celebration. The word "preface" comes from the Latin *praefatio*, made up of the prefix *pre-* ("before") and *facies* ("face"). Since we have lifted our hearts to God, the priest is now saying the preface before the very face of God; the ancient tradition of facing east during the Mass adds to this symbolism.

The Preface ends by mentioning that we are joining the angels and all the heavenly host in their unending hymn of praise.

Holy, Holy, Holy

Sanctus

This is the second time during the Mass when we join in singing the words of the angels. The first time, in the *Gloria*, we echoed what the angels sang temporally, when Christ was born on earth; now we echo the *Sanctus*, the hymn they sing eternally in Heaven:

> **Sanctus, Sanctus, Sanctus Dóminus Deus Sábaoth.**
> **Pleni sunt cæli et terra glória tua.**
> **Hosánna in excélsis.**

» Holy, Holy, Holy Lord God of hosts.   *Ps. 89:8; Isa. 6:3; Rev. 4:8*
  Heaven and earth are full of your glory.   *Num. 14:21; Acts 7:55; Rev. 15:8*
  Hosanna in the highest.

The old English translation rendered the Latin-and-Hebrew expression *"Dominus Deus Sabaoth"* as "Lord God of power and might,"[2] but that did not do justice to this rich Scriptural title for God, "Lord God of hosts." This title (along with "Lord of hosts" and "God of hosts") occurs nearly 300 times in Scripture.

The word "host" here does not refer to the Eucharistic host;[3] rather, this word means "a multitude" and "an army." The Lord commands the heavenly host of angels, and the archangel Michael is recognized as the "captain" of this host. (cf. Jude 1:9; Rev. 12:7) This military language reminds us that we are waging a spiritual battle (cf. 2 Cor. 10:3-4) with God and His saints and angels fighting with us; we must be equipped for such a battle. (cf. Eph. 6:10-17)

We pray in adoration of the triple-holiness of God. The repetition of "holy" three times is a Hebraism. There are not separate words to express a superlative in Hebrew; instead, the word "holy" is doubled to speak of the "holy of holies" (the most holy place in the Temple) and it is tripled to speak of the most holy One: God alone, as Isaiah and St. John testify to. (cf. Isa. 6:3; Rev. 4:8) The triple invocation of God as holy also takes on a new meaning with the revelation of the Trinity: we are saying that Father, Son, and Holy Spirit are all holy, and equally so.

To this confession of holiness is added a statement of wonder and awe at the surpassing glory of God which is seen in all of His creation. Once again, as in the Creed, we affirm that God is the God Who created the invisible *and* visible world, and that His physical creation shows forth His glory. It is also a challenge for us to manifest that glory of God in the world. We'll come back to that when we pray the Our Father.

The words of the *Hosanna* are explained next.

Benedictus

To the song of angels is attached the song of men, the *Benedictus*, the words of Psalm 118, which the people of Jerusalem shouted joyfully when Jesus entered the city on what we now celebrate as Palm Sunday:

---

[2] The current translation tends to associate the word "Lord" with "Holy, Holy, Holy," leaving "God of power and might" as a separate phrase, rather than treating "Lord God" as a whole.

[3] The word "host" used to describe both the unconsecrated and consecrated bread comes from the Latin word *hostia* which means "victim."

Benedíctus qui venit in nómine Dómini.
Hosánna in excélsis.

Blessed is he who comes in the name of the Lord.   *Ps. 118:26; Phil. 2:11*

Hosanna in the highest.   *Ps. 118:25; Matt. 21:9; John 12:13*

The city of Jerusalem (on Palm Sunday) spoke of Jesus as "he who comes in the name of the Lord." Little did they realize that Jesus was coming in *His own name*, since Jesus is Lord! The cry of *Hosanna* (related to the Hebrew word *hoshea*, "savior") is at once a word of praise and a shout for salvation. It acknowledges God as Savior while calling upon Him to save His people; it means, "Please, save [us]!" or "Hasten to save [us]!"

When the people of Jerusalem shouted and greeted Jesus in this way, the Pharisees were angered and told Jesus to silence His disciples. The Lord responded with these words: "I tell you, if these were silent, the very stones would cry out." (Luke 19:40) G.K. Chesterton, a well-known Catholic author of the early 20th century, once wrote that "Christ prophesied the whole of Gothic architecture" by his words:

> Under the impulse of His spirit arose like a clamorous chorus the façades of the medieval cathedrals, thronged with shouting faces and open mouths. The prophecy has fulfilled itself: the very stones cry out. (*Orthodoxy*, chapter 7)

He meant that the architecture of Gothic cathedrals is such that, even when there is no one in them, they seem to be singing praise to God.

The only other place in Scripture in which stones are prophesied to speak is in the book of the prophet Habbakuk:

> Woe to him who gets evil gain for his house, to set his nest on high, to be safe from the reach of harm! You have devised shame to your house by cutting off many peoples; you have forfeited your life. For *the stone will cry out from the wall*, and the beam from the woodwork respond. (Hab. 2:9-11)

The theme of both of these passages is that the voice of God's faithful, whether they are singing praise or crying out against injustice, can never be silenced by man, even if that voice is "cut off."

With these words, we are praying to Jesus Christ, Who comes to us in no other name than His own, to save us, and we praise Him for the salvation He has already won for us. In this moment, let us not be silent, that we should be ashamed when the rest of God's creation makes up for our timidity.

After this joyful hymn, we kneel as the Eucharistic Prayer is prayed.

Consecration

At the end of the first half of the Eucharistic Prayer is the consecration, by which the bread and wine become the Body and Blood of our Lord. This is the *source* and *summit* of the whole Mass. It is a pious practice to make some silent prayer when the priest elevates the Host and Chalice for adoration. (The priest himself genuflects in private adoration after he has placed them back on the altar.) Saying "My Lord and my God!" like St. Thomas the doubter (John 20:28), or "We adore you, O Christ, and we bless you..." are common prayers.

The change which takes place on the altar is not detectable to our eyes and other senses. St. Augustine proposed the obvious question:

> A thought such as this could come about in the mind of any one of you: "We learned from where Our Lord Jesus Christ took flesh: the Virgin Mary. ... On the day he willed, he ascended into Heaven: his body, lifted up, is there. ... How, then, is the bread his body? And the chalice, or rather that which the chalice holds, how is it his blood?"

> For just that reason, brethren, such things are called "sacraments" because in them *one* thing is *seen*, but *another* thing is *understood*. That which is seen has a tangible appearance; that which is understood bears spiritual fruit.

In the sacraments, we *observe* one thing (e.g. water being poured over someone, rings being put on fingers) but we *recognize* a greater and deeper reality (e.g. the cleansing of sin, a man and a woman vowing fidelity and entering a marital covenant). What is understood in the bread and wine which become the Body and Blood? St. Augustine does not describe transubstantiation to the new Christians, but relates the Eucharist to *them*:

> Therefore, if you wish to understand the body of Christ, pay attention to the Apostle saying to the faithful, "You, moreover, are the body of Christ, and its members." (1 Cor. 12:27) If, therefore, you are the body of Christ and its members, *your* mystery is placed on the Lord's table.

In this way, the miracle of the Eucharist is *our* miracle. It is truly the Body and Blood of Christ which are present under the appearances of bread and wine. But this body which is veiled to us is not just the Real Presence of Jesus Christ, but also that body to which Jesus is mystically joined: the Church. In this way, the bread and wine which represented our offerings and our lives are changed and elevated beyond simple "representation" to the level of a true sacramental *sign* of each of us, united in the one body of the Church.

Then St. Augustine discusses the *elements* of bread and wine: why did Jesus choose these two as the perpetual sign of His body and ours? He brings up the words of St. Paul, "Because there is one bread, we who are many are one body." (1 Cor. 10:17)

> Understand and rejoice: unity, truth, piety, love. "One bread" – what is that one bread? It is "the one body" which we the "many" are. Bring this to the forefront of your mind: bread is not made from a single grain, but from many.
>
> When you were being exorcised, it is as though you were being ground up. When you were baptized, it is as though you were mixed together [into dough]. When you received the fire of the Holy Spirit, it is as though you were being baked. ...
>
> As many grains are mixed into one that it might be the visible appearance of bread, just as if to bring about that which the Holy Scripture says concerning the faithful, "They were one soul and one heart in God" (cf. Acts 4:32), so too with the wine: brethren, recall from what wine is made: many grapes hang in a bunch, but the juice of the grapes is combined into one.

Not only are bread and wine richly symbolic of "the stuff of life," but as St. Augustine points out, they are both produced in the same manner: many grains are crushed and combined into one loaf; many grapes are crushed and poured into one cup. This dying to self (cf. Luke 9:24) is a personal, daily "martyrdom" where we choose Christ over ourselves and show our commitment to be a member of His *one* body, His Church.

He concludes the allegory of the grapes and the faithful by alluding to the words of Christ in John 15:1-8:

> Even thus Christ the Lord signified us, and willed us to belong to him...

Jesus is the vine (of grapes, naturally) and we are the branches. The same "blood" that flows through the vine flows also into each of its branches that those branches might "bear much fruit." (John 15:8) We must abide in Christ to receive His blood by which He abides in us. The vine and the branches must be together: no branch can *live*, let alone bear fruit, apart from the vine.

The Mystery of Faith

After the consecration, the priest says *"Mysterium fidei"* — that is, "The mystery of faith" — referring to the miracle of transubstantiation which has just taken place on the altar. In response to this great miracle, we say or sing an acclamation (formerly called the "Memorial Acclamation").

In the Extraordinary Form of the Mass, it is not uncommon for the *Sanctus* (with one *Hosanna*) to be sung as the Roman Canon begins, and the *Benedictus* (starting with "Blessed is he...") to be sung after the words of consecration. There is no acclamation in the Extraordinary Form of the Mass, but the words of the *Benedictus* are very powerful in meaning when sung just after Christ has been made present on the altar in the Blessed Sacrament.

In the Ordinary Form of the Mass, there are three acclamations which can be sung after the consecration.[4] Each of these texts is heavily Scriptural; two are derived from the first letter to the Corinthians, where we find St. Paul's Eucharistic theology.

We Proclaim Your Death...

Mortem tuam annuntiámus, Dómine,
et tuam resurrectiónem confitémur, donec vénias.

» We proclaim your death, O Lord,   *1 Cor. 11:26*
» and profess your Resurrection until you come again.   *Acts 2:32*

This prayer reminds us of the perpetual mission of the Church: never to cease proclaiming the death and the Resurrection of our Savior. That *is* the Gospel. One of the ways the Church proclaims the Gospel is by celebrating the Eucharist, which contains and makes present the whole Paschal mystery. In celebrating the Mass, we intimately encounter the Gospel, but this encounter does not end after Mass is over (as we will see when we look at the Concluding Rite).

---

[4] The familiar "Christ has died, Christ is risen, Christ will come again" is not included. This acclamation was an addition to the English translation of the previous edition of the Missal, and is not found in the Latin text of the 2002 Missal nor the new English translation. The USCCB has requested an indult for its inclusion in the new translation, but as of the printing of this book, that request has not been answered. Also missing is the acclamation "Dying you destroyed our death, rising you restored our life: Lord Jesus, come in glory," which did not correspond to any of the Latin acclamations either, but was derived from the text of the Preface for Easter I (*Qui mortem nostram moriéndo destrúxit, et vitam resurgéndo reparávit*).

When We Eat This Bread...

Quotiescúmque manducámus panem hunc et cálicem bíbimus, mortem tuam annuntiámus, Dómine, donec vénias.

When we eat this Bread and drink this Cup,   *1 Cor. 11:26*
» we proclaim your death, O Lord, until you come again.

The words of this prayer are almost directly out of St. Paul's letter: "As often as you eat this bread and drink the chalice, you proclaim the Lord's death until he comes." (1 Cor. 11:26) This means that the very action of consecrating the Eucharist and receiving Holy Communion is a *sign* of the death of the Lord; the Church recognizes that this sign, called a sacrament, makes present the mystery being signified. In the language of the Catechism, "The Eucharist is thus a sacrifice because it *re-presents* (makes present) the sacrifice of the cross, because it is its *memorial* and because it applies its *fruit*." (*Catechism* 1366)

The separate consecration of the bread and the wine is a sign of the true death of Jesus Christ: His blood was separated from His body. He gave up His body for us, and poured out His blood for the remission of sins. That, in itself, *announces* the death of the Lord. When we go a step further and actually consume His Body and Blood, we are fulfilling the command He gave at the Last Supper, because it is the sacrificial banquet in which we ratify our membership in the new covenant formed in Christ's blood.

Save Us, Savior of the World...

**Salvátor mundi, salva nos,
qui per crucem et resurrectiónem tuam liberásti nos.**

» Save us, Savior of the world,   *John 4:42; 2 Tim. 4:18; Heb. 9:28*
» for by your Cross *Wis. 14:7; 1 Cor. 1:18; Gal. 6:14; Col. 1:20*
and Resurrection you have set us free. *John 8:32; Rom. 4:25; Gal. 5:1*

The old English translation of this acclamation was lacking in one thing, shown in bold in this comparison:

Old Translation	New Translation
Lord, by your cross and resurrection,	**Save us**, Savior of the world,
you have set us free:	for by your Cross and
you are the Savior of the world.	Resurrection you have set us free.

The acclamation has a cry of *Hosanna* in it: *Salva nos*, "Save us!" Even though we have been "set free" by Christ's death and Resurrection by which He won us our salvation, we are still dependent on Christ for that salvation. The Biblical picture of salvation is a continuum: we *have been* saved (cf. Rom. 8:24; Eph. 2:8), we *are being* saved (cf. 1 Cor. 1:18), and we *hope to be* saved. (cf. Rom. 5:9-10) For this reason, at the same time that we acknowledge having been set free by Jesus, we call out to Him with the prayer of Israel, the prayer of every sinner, and especially of St. Peter: "Lord, save me!" (Matt. 14:30)

In a chapter of the Book of Wisdom which speaks about Noah and the ark, there is a prophetic verse which finds its fulfillment in the Cross of Christ:

> It is your will that works of your wisdom should not be without effect; therefore men trust their lives even to the smallest piece of wood, and passing through the billows on a raft they come safely to land. For even in the beginning, when arrogant giants were perishing, the hope of the world took refuge on a raft, and guided by your hand left to the world the seed of a new generation. For *blessed is the wood by which righteousness comes.* (Wis. 14:5-7)

While the author was concerned with something in the past, the Holy Spirit gave him words which had a far deeper meaning. What makes this a surprising prophecy is that crucifixion was *not* a Jewish punishment (which is why the Sanhedrin had to bring Jesus to Pilate) and that the hanging of a body upon a tree was seen as the absolute *antithesis* to righteousness and blessing:

> If a man has committed a crime punishable by death and he is put to death, and you hang him on a tree, his body shall not remain all night upon the tree, but you shall bury him the same day, for *a hanged man is accursed by God; you shall not defile your land* which the LORD your God gives you for an inheritance. (Deut. 21:22-23)

St. Paul reinterprets the curse of Deuteronomy, saying that Christ turned the curse into a blessing: "Christ redeemed us from the curse of the law, having become a curse for us – for it is written, 'Cursed be every one who hangs on a tree' – that in Christ Jesus the blessing of Abraham might come upon the Gentiles, that we might receive the promise of the Spirit through faith." (Gal. 3:13-14) God waited for the right time for the fulfillment of all these prophecies, when Israel would be under the occupation of a society which had crucifixion as a punishment, among other things; this is why it is said that God sent His Son "when the time had fully come." (Gal. 4:4)[5]

The Mystery of Faith

This mystery of faith involves us, too, for the Body of Christ is at once the Eucharist on the altar and the Church: as St. Augustine said, the mystery taking place on the altar is *our* mystery as well. In the change of bread and wine into the Body and Blood of Christ, we recognize the change taking place in us as we "with unveiled face, beholding the glory of the Lord, are being changed into his likeness from one degree of glory to another." (2 Cor. 3:18) This change culminates in the resurrection of our bodies to their eternal glorified state, when Christ "will change our lowly body to be like his glorious body." (Phil. 3:21; cf. 1 Cor. 15:51-52)

Parousia[6]

The liturgical year begins with the season of Advent. This word comes from the Latin *advenio* which means "to arrive; to come." In every liturgy, we remember the first advent of the Lord (His Incarnation) as we look forward to His second advent, as Eucharistic Prayer III makes clear:

> Therefore, O Lord, as we celebrate the memorial of the saving Passion of your Son, his wondrous Resurrection and Ascension into heaven, and *as we look forward to his second coming*, we offer you in thanksgiving this holy and living sacrifice.

The Greek word *parousia* means both "arrival" and "presence." Jesus used the word when He said, "For as the lightning comes from the east and shines as far as the west, so will be *the coming* of the Son of man." (Matt. 24:27)[7]

The resurrection of the dead is a future reality, but it is anticipated now through Baptism: "you were buried with him in baptism, in which *you were also raised* with him..." (Col. 2:12) In a similar manner, although there will be a definitive *parousia*, the "second coming" of the Lord at the

---

[5] These words can also be translated "in the fullness of time."

[6] This section is inspired by the essay "Come Again?" by Scott Hahn, in *Catholic for a Reason III: Scripture and the Mystery of the Mass* (pp. 31-47), and by his book, *The Lamb's Supper*.

[7] The Mass and Divine Liturgy are historically celebrated facing the east, the direction which the Lord identifies with His return. Perhaps this is another connection between His Eucharistic *parousia* ("presence") and His future *parousia* ("coming").

end of time, the Eucharist is an anticipatory manifestation of that *parousia* here and now. Consider this hymn from the ancient Liturgy of St. James:

> Let all mortal flesh be silent, and stand with fear and trembling, and meditate nothing earthly within itself: For the King of kings and Lord of lords, *Christ our God, comes forward* to be sacrificed, and to be given for food to the faithful...[8]

Another ancient prayer associated with the Eucharist, found in the *Didache*,[9] uses the word *Maranatha*. This term is found in one of St. Paul's letters, translated in the RSV as "Our Lord, come!" (1 Cor. 16:22) It is a cry for the *parousia*; its proximity to the Eucharist is evidence of the connection which the early Church made between the two. The concept is found in the modern Roman liturgy in the two acclamations based on 1 Corinthians 11:26 ("... until you come again").

The coming of the Lord is described in Scripture as being glorious. (cf. Matt. 16:27; 2 Th. 1:9-10) In His Eucharistic *parousia*, the glory of the Lord is hidden beneath the appearances of bread and wine; in His future *parousia*, we will see His glory:

> The Church knows that the Lord comes even now in his Eucharist and that he is there in our midst. However, his presence is veiled. Therefore we celebrate the Eucharist "awaiting the blessed hope and the coming of our Savior, Jesus Christ..." (*Catechism* 1404, quoting the *Roman Missal* 126, embolism after the Our Father: *exspectantes beatam spem et adventum Salvatoris nostri Jesu Christi*; cf. Titus 2:13.)

Another link between the Eucharistic liturgy and the *parousia* comes from the words of Jesus Christ himself:

> "Behold, your house is forsaken and desolate. For I tell you, you will not see me again, until you say, 'Blessed is he who comes in the name of the Lord.'" (Matt. 23:38-39)

Scott Hahn finds it fitting that the Church places those words "on our lips just moments before the Eucharistic consecration in the Mass, just moments before our Lord's Eucharistic *parousia*."

"Amen."

The *Gloria* (from chapter 5) is called the "major doxology" (which means "words of glory"). The *Gloria Patri* ("Glory to the Father...") is called

---

[8] This ancient liturgical hymn is the basis for the hymn "Let All Mortal Flesh Keep Silence."
[9] "The Teaching of the Twelve Apostles," dated to the late first or early second century.

the "minor doxology." The *Per ipsum* ("Through him...") at the end of the Eucharistic Prayer is the "Eucharistic doxology," in which the priest offers glory and honor to the Father through, in, and with the Son, in the unity of the Holy Spirit. We respond with a hearty "Amen!"

To St. Augustine, saying "Amen" to a prayer is like appending your signature to a document. When his successor was taking over as Bishop of Hippo (A.D. 426), St. Augustine gave a speech, ending it this way:

> I see that I have now transacted with you all the business necessary in the matter for which I called you together. The last thing I have to ask is, that as many of you as are able be pleased to *subscribe your names to this record.* At this point I require a response from you. Let me have it: *show your assent* by some acclamations. (Letter CCXIII)

This subscription of names, this assent, was shown by shouts of "Amen" among acclamations. The analogy here is an important one. How often do we sign our names to contracts without actually *reading* them? We know we shouldn't, but we do it anyway. Prayer should not be like a document we skim through (if we read it at all) and sloppily scribble our signatures on.

We say "Amen" at the end of the Eucharistic Prayer to show our personal assent to the prayer of the priest. It also concludes our own personal "Eucharistic" prayer, as we join ourselves to Christ on the altar and ask the Father to accept us with His Son. But this "Amen" pales in comparison to the one we'll say in a few minutes, as the Eucharist is brought down to us from the altar and given to us, when the Lord of the Universe comes to abide in us.

In the Extraordinary Form of the Mass, the Eucharistic Prayer is said in almost complete silence. In the Ordinary Form, it is spoken aloud. But we must always remember that the priest is not speaking to *us* but praying to God. This can be made more clear when the Liturgy of the Eucharist is celebrated *ad orientem*, that is, with the priest standing on the same side of the altar as the congregation, facing the same direction as them. This posture of prayer is common to both the Eastern and Western Church.

While it is good to listen to the words of the prayer, don't get so caught up that you simply become a spectator to the Eucharistic Prayer. Learn to pay attention to the prayer while meditating on the Eucharist and offering your own internal prayer, similar to praying the Rosary, in which one contemplates the mysteries of Christ while praying the "Hail Mary" at the same time. This meditation and contemplation reaches its height as we pray as one family the words of the prayer Christ gave us, and prepare to receive Him in Holy Communion.

Questions for Reflection

1) **Interpret:** How is the use of incense (found in the Church and in Jewish Temple worship) a sign of lifting our hearts and hands to the Lord?

2) **Interpret:** Eucharistic Prayer I (the Roman Canon) connects the Eucharist to the sacrifices of Abel (cf. Gen. 4:4) and Abraham (cf. Gen. 22:13-14) and the bread and wine offered by the priest Melchizedek. (cf. Gen. 14:18-20) How is the offering of the Eucharist similar to those? How does it surpass them?

3) **Interpret:** How is the Eucharist a surpassing fulfillment of the Passover sacrifice?

4) **Explain:** Why does the *Sanctus-Benedictus* draw on the heavenly hymn of the angels and the song of Jerusalem? What do those two places (Heaven and Jerusalem) have to do with salvation?

5) **Explain:** Why do we kneel for the Eucharistic Prayer? During the words of consecration, the priest leans over the altar. What might he be imitating in doing so? Why does the priest say "This is *my* body" rather than "This is *his* body"?

6) **Relate:** How do the acclamations at the Consecration remind us of the mission of the Church? How is the Eucharist a summary of that mission?

7) **Relate:** How are the other sacraments (Baptism, Confirmation, Confession, Holy Orders, Matrimony, and Anointing of the Sick) related to the Eucharist?

*For you are our Father, though Abraham does not know us
and Israel does not acknowledge us; you, O LORD,
are our Father, our Redeemer from of old is your name.*
(Isaiah 63:16)

*Because you are sons, God has sent the Spirit of his Son
into our hearts, crying, "Abba! Father!" So through God
you are no longer a slave but a son, and if a son then an heir.*
(Galatians 4:6-7)

11

Communion Rite

COMMUNION IN THE Church is more than just a sacrament. The word comes from the Greek word *koinonia*. This word means "fellowship; unity, community; sharing." In the early Church "all who believed *were together* and *had all things in common*, and they sold their possessions and goods and distributed them to all, as any had need ... [and they] were *of one heart and soul*, and no one said that any of the things which he possessed was his own." (Acts 2:44-45; 4:32) When we receive Holy Communion, it is a sign of being in union with Christ and His Church. This union is not a mere human sentiment, but a deep spiritual reality which calls us to be "of one heart and soul." This is why a Catholic may not receive Communion in a Protestant community, and why (except in extraordinary circumstances) a Protestant cannot receive Communion in a Catholic church: although Catholics and Protestants may share *some* beliefs, a Protestant is not in full communion with the Church, and therefore (sadly) not in full communion with Christ.

This communion with the Church extends to communion with all who belong to the Church. This is known as fellowship or partnership. St. John tells us that "if we say we have *fellowship with him* while we walk in darkness, we lie and do not live according to the truth; but if we walk in the light, as he is in the light, we have *fellowship with one another*, and the blood of Jesus his Son cleanses us from all sin." (1 John 1:6-7) If we are in partnership with Christ, we must also be in partnership with those who are *in* Christ. This is manifested through sharing those blessings and gifts which God has bestowed on us:

> God has so composed the body, giving the greater honor to the inferior part, that there may be no discord in the body, but that *the members may have the same care for one another*. If one member suffers, all suffer together; if one member is honored, all rejoice together. (1 Cor. 12:24-26)

Through the prayers of the Communion Rite, we acknowledge that our brothers and sisters in the Church have the *right* to communion with us, and that we have an obligation to show that partnership, unity, and sharing with them.

"Our Father"

The first manifestation of that communion is in the prayer that Jesus gave to us as the *ideal* prayer and as the *model* for prayer. Emboldened by Jesus Christ, through Whom we have gained divine adoption, we dare to call God *Abba*, "Father" – and not just my Father or your Father, but *our* Father. Because Jesus taught his disciples this prayer, it is also called the "Lord's Prayer." In this prayer, we ask for the coming of God's kingdom and the accomplishment of His will, language which calls to mind the Church's longing for the *parousia* of the Lord.

Tertullian – a Latin theologian of the late 2nd century, and the man who coined the term *trinitas* for describing God as Father, Son, and Holy Spirit – wrote that "truly in this prayer is expressed a summary of the whole Gospel." (*De Oratione*, I; cf. *Catechism* 2761) If we remember that the Our Father is a prayer meant to form us in Christ every time we pray it (like the *Gloria* and the Creed), then we can see in each petition a call to communion with God and His Church.

The Our Father has seven petitions, which have been numbered for convenience. We will look at the prayer in two parts: the first three petitions as a unit, and then the last four petitions as a unit.

Pater noster, qui es in cælis: sanctificétur nomen tuum; advéniat regnum tuum; fiat volúntas tua, sicut in cælo, et in terra.

Our Father, who art in heaven:	*Matt. 6:9-13; Luke 11:2-4*
(1) hallowed be thy name;	*Neh. 9:5; Ps. 113:2; Luke 1:49; John 12:28*
(2) thy kingdom come;	*Mark 1:15; Luke 10:9; Rev. 12:10*
(3) thy will be done on earth as it is in heaven.	*Matt. 7:21; Acts 21:14*

The prayer begins by addressing God the Father; the first three petitions are focused on His glory rather than on us. This serves two purposes: first, it reminds us that when we pray to God, we should praise and honor Him before we speak of ourselves and our needs; second, these first petitions inform our souls of the proper disposition for prayer.

Our Father in Heaven

We address God the Father, Whom Jesus revealed to us as *Abba*, which means "Daddy." This familial title would have been scandalous to any 1ˢᵗ-century Jew; only rarely in their Scriptures (fewer than a dozen times[1]) is God referred to as "Father" and then it as "Father" and not as "Daddy." St. Paul explains that it is through our relationship with Jesus, the only Son of God, that we can call upon God in such a familiar way: we were born of the lineage of Adam as "children of wrath" (Eph. 2:3), but have received "adoption as sons" (Gal. 4:5-6; cf. Rom. 8:15-17) by our Baptism.

Because God is Spirit, the uncreated Creator, He Who is outside of time and space, He transcends His creation: we profess our Father to be "in heaven." At the same time, God is immanent and comes close to us through His Son and the Holy Spirit. This apparent contradiction is not a problem, but rather a display of His glorious providence. God is not an aloof, impenetrable, absolutely unknowable, and unrevealing god who can only be seen as some "higher power" out there somewhere; but neither is He some "energy" or "force" that flows through everything in such a way that any other man, or an animal, or a tree, or even a rock is to be regarded and revered as if it were God Himself.

Instead, God is above and outside all of His creation, but enters it through revelation (and in a unique and unrepeatable way through His

---

[1] Cf. Tob. 13:4; Ps. 68:5; 89:26; Wis. 14:3; Sir. 23:1, 4; 51:10; Isa. 63:16; 64:8; Jer. 3:19. There are other places in Scripture where attributes of a father are given to God, such as in Hos. 11:1-4.

Son); and while His Spirit vivifies all creation and keeps it in existence, the creation is *distinct* from its Creator. Animals, plants, rocks, water, and dirt are creatures of God, but their purpose is to serve us and to glorify God, *not* to receive glory due only to Him. We are temples of the Holy Spirit, but it is the Spirit Who is to be worshiped, not ourselves!

Hallowed be Thy Name

In the first petition, we pray that God's name would be hallowed, or "sanctified; made holy." The opposite of this petition is profaning the name of the Lord, also known as *blasphemy*.[2] In one of the readings from the Easter Vigil (from Ezekiel 36:16-28), God tells Israel that because of their conduct which had caused Him to scatter them as punishment, they ended up profaning His name, because the other nations ridiculed them by saying: "These are the people of the LORD, and yet they had to go out of his land." (Ezek. 36:20) In response, God promised to gather them together again, not because of *their* merits or glory or greatness, but for the sake of His holy name, so that all the other nations would come to know the holiness of His great name.

This petition is fulfilled in two ways. First, God Himself glorifies and hallows His holy name when He manifests His greatness through miracles and mighty acts of salvation, as He did for Israel in the reading from the Easter Vigil. (cf. Ps. 115:1; Dan. 3:43) Second, it is fulfilled when we do good works which lead others to give glory, not to us, but to God. (cf. Matt. 5:16) By praying this, we profess a desire to manifest the holiness of God's name to all people in all nations. (cf. *Catechism* 2858)

Thy Kingdom Come

In the second petition, we pray for the coming of God's kingdom. This kingdom was proclaimed in the preaching of St. John the Baptist who told all who would hear him, "Repent, for the kingdom of heaven is at hand." (Matt. 3:2) St. Matthew calls the preaching of Jesus "the gospel of the *kingdom*." (Matt. 4:23) This kingdom is in our midst because of the presence of Christ (cf. Luke 17:21) and is present on earth mystically in the Church, as a plant is in its seed. (cf. *Catechism* 669)

---

2 The book of Leviticus identifies three particular offences which profane God's name: the sacrificing of children to false gods, specifically Molech (cf. Lev. 18:21; 20:3); swearing falsely by His name (cf. Lev. 19:12); and stealing things which are dedicated to the Lord. (cf. Lev. 22:2)

While we pray for the Lord's return, we are also praying that the kingdom, present in the Church, might grow. This happens through the Church's mission to preach the Gospel and bring souls to Christ through His Church. It would be un-Christian to pray for the return of the Lord (with the ensuing final judgment) without also fulfilling our part in the mission of the Church to bring all men to salvation. (cf. *Catechism* 2859)

Thy Will be Done

In the third petition, we pray that God's will would be accomplished. God wants all of humanity to be saved (cf. 1 Tim. 2:3-4), and He loves us with a love that exceeds all our imagination. (cf. 1 John 4:9-10) It follows, then, that all of God's will can be summed up in these words: "if God so loved us, we also ought to love one another." (1 John 4:11) Our Lord did much to teach His disciples the importance of loving one another. Two of His parables, in particular, that make this point quite plain are the Good Samaritan (cf. Luke 10:25-37) and the Judgment of the Nations. (cf. Matt. 25:31-46) These two parables convey God's answer, through His Son Jesus Christ, to Cain's selfish question: "Am I my brother's keeper?" (Gen. 4:9) God answers *Yes!* with His Son, Who is the *Amen*, the *Yes*, the faithful and true witness. (cf. Rev. 3:14)

God's will is not perfectly accomplished on earth because of sin. In order to accomplish His will, we need to conform ourselves to Christ and live as members of His kingdom, where His law is love. Christ came to earth *not to be served* but *to serve*: in Him is Kingship perfected, in that He loves His subjects so dearly and truly that He ministers to them and dies for them. We, who have been baptized into this Kingship, exercise it when we serve as He served, when we love as He loved. In this way, we will give glory to God's name and we will bring about a daily *parousia* by manifesting the love of Christ to everyone we come in contact with. We pray in this petition that our will might be united to Christ's, so that the salvation He won might be known in the world. (cf. *Catechism* 2860)

In Heaven and on Earth

All three of these first petitions can rightfully lay claim to the phrase "on earth as it is in heaven." In Heaven, God's name is perfectly hallowed, His kingdom is realized in His saints and angels already worshiping Him in the new Jerusalem, and His will is perfectly accomplished. On earth, however, the fulfillment of these three petitions is impeded daily by sin.

By saying "on earth as it is in heaven," we are recognizing that the model of perfection is not some earthly utopia, but God's kingdom in Heaven: there is no secular community that can achieve what is possible through the heavenly kingdom, nor a human power that can supplant the power of Jesus Christ, true man *and* true God.

Panem nostrum cotidiánum da nobis hódie;
et dimítte nobis débita nostra,
sicut et nos dimíttimus debitóribus nostris;
et ne nos indúcas in tentatiónem; sed líbera nos a malo.

(4) Give us this day our daily bread,   *Ex. 16:4,31; Acts 2:46*
(5) and forgive us our trespasses,   *Matt. 6:14-15; 18:21-35; Col. 3:13*
as we forgive those who trespass against us;
(6) and lead us not into temptation;   *1 Cor. 10:13; Heb. 2:18; Jas. 1:13*
(7) but deliver us from evil.   *Luke 1:74; Gal. 1:4; Col. 1:3; 1 Th. 1:10*

The first three petitions spoke of God's glory, His Kingdom, and His will. By participating in the mission of the Church (which is the mission of Christ), we are bringing about those three things. Our participation is the subject of the next four petitions. We call upon God as our provider, our forgiver, our protector, and our deliverer, so that our needs may be met as we work towards the fulfillment of this mission.

Our Daily Bread

When St. Jerome was translating the Gospels from Greek into Latin, he did something peculiar when he came to Matthew 6:11 and Luke 11:3. These two verses use the same Greek word (*epiousion*) in describing the bread we ask from our Father; this word comes from *epi-* ("over, super") and *ousion* ("essence", remember *homoousion* from the Creed?). This word only appears in Scripture here, and has only been found in one other Greek text *ever*. St. Jerome translated that single Greek word with two different Latin words: in Matthew he used *supersubstantialem* (a direct and literal translation), which means "life-giving, necessary to support life," but in Luke he used *cotidianum*, which means "daily, everyday."

Both translations are appropriate, and the meaning of the prayer is made much clearer when both translations are known. In order for us to carry out the mission of the Church, we need to be sustained daily by

God. We depend on God for our daily life and sustenance (bread, water, shelter, light, etc.), and the Incarnation of His Son was necessary to provide for us the heavenly Bread, the Bread of Life, which is truly life-giving and which the Church provides for us daily. (cf. *Catechism* 2861) This petition is only offered *after* the Eucharist has been consecrated and offered to God in the Eucharistic Prayer: the Eucharist is a sacrifice *first*, and a sacred banquet *second*.

Forgive Us as We Forgive

In the fifth petition, we ask God to forgive us, but we admit that we are *only* to be forgiven to the same extent and degree that we forgive others! Because the preaching of the Gospel by both John the Baptist and Jesus begins with the word "repent" (Matt. 3:2; 4:17), this forgiveness (received and given to others) is necessary to authentically carry out the Church's mission. Jesus elaborated on the importance of showing forgiveness to others on more than one occasion:

> "Blessed are the merciful, for they shall obtain mercy." (Matt. 5:7)
>
> "For if you forgive men their trespasses, your heavenly Father also will forgive you; but if you do not forgive men their trespasses, neither will your Father forgive your trespasses." (Matt. 6:14-15)
>
> "So also my heavenly Father will do to every one of you, if you do not forgive your brother from your heart." (Matt. 18:35)
>
> "And whenever you stand praying, forgive, if you have anything against any one; so that your Father also who is in heaven may forgive you your trespasses." (Mark 11:25)
>
> "Forgive, and you will be forgiven." (Luke 6:37)

The desire for forgiveness is rooted in the eschatological and Eucharistic dimensions of the Lord's *parousia*: eschatological because we do not know when Christ is returning (cf. Mark 13:32-37), and Eucharistic because we must be sure we do not receive Communion in an unworthy manner. (cf. 1 Cor. 11:27-29). There is never any reason to delay coming to Him and pleading for His mercy which He bestows so generously.

God calls us to cooperate with Him in the mission of His Son. This petition is fulfilled by Christ when it is fulfilled by us. We are compelled to show mercy even to our enemies. (cf. Matt. 5:44) In doing so, they may come to learn the great love and mercy of God and turn to Him. It is by showing mercy that our hearts and souls can receive the perfect mercy of God, and we learn to show this mercy by following the example of Christ. (cf. *Catechism* 2862)

Trespasses and Debts

The word *debita*, which is translated in the liturgy as "trespasses," can be rendered (some would argue more accurately) as "debts." When we sin against God (or anyone), we are in a sense "trespassing" against Him; we are transgressing His divine law. The Catholic Church's theology of the atonement – which was masterfully articulated at the beginning of the 12th century by St. Anselm of Canterbury in *Cur Deus Homo* ("Why God Became Man"), and later by St. Thomas Aquinas – posits that we owe a debt of honor to God, and that sin incurs yet another debt, one of moral injustice.

Jesus gave a parable in which He illustrated two ways of settling a debt: paying it or forgiving it. (cf. Matt. 18:21-35) To forgive a debt is to free the debtor from his obligation to settle the debt. This merciful act is strongly tied to two customs of the law of Israel: every seventh year, debts between Israelites were remitted (cf. Deut. 15), and every fiftieth year was *a year of Jubilee* when slaves were set free. (cf. Lev. 25) This Jubilee year was mentioned in a prophecy of Isaiah which Jesus fulfilled in His reading of it at the synagogue in His hometown of Nazareth:

> He opened the book and found the place where it was written, "The Spirit of the Lord is upon me, because he has anointed me to preach good news to the poor. He has sent me to proclaim release to the captives and recovering of sight to the blind, to set at liberty those who are oppressed, *to proclaim the acceptable year of the Lord.*" And he closed the book, and gave it back to the attendant, and sat down; and the eyes of all in the synagogue were fixed on him. And he began to say to them, "Today this scripture has been fulfilled in your hearing." (Luke 4:17-21; cf. Isa. 42:6-7; 61:1-2)

Seen in this light, the Our Father is a prayer of release, a prayer which calls us to make present in our daily lives the Jubilee inaugurated by Christ. (cf. *Catechism* 2449, 2845)

Temptation

It is important to distinguish between *trials* (which are necessary for our spiritual growth) and *temptations* (which are occasions for sin). God gives us tests for our benefit, that we may come to a better understanding of the depth of our faith in Him and His love for us. (cf. Gen. 22:1-18) But Satan tempts us by striking at our weaknesses to cause us to doubt the worth of our faith in God and His love for us. (cf. Job 1:9-11) As we live out the mission of the Church, we can be sure that Satan will try to make us falter, so as to make the Gospel message we preach seem like empty words; this is why we must pray for strength in the face of temptation.

The translation of the sixth petition from Greek into English is not easy, because the phrase means both "do not let us *yield* to temptation" and "do not allow us to *enter* into temptation." (*Catechism* 2846) God is our protector when we are tempted; seeking to cling to God, we ask for the necessary spiritual strength: in Scripture, this is called "endurance" or "perseverance." (cf. *Catechism* 2863)

Deliver Us

One can be delivered *into* the hands of one's enemies, or one can be delivered *from* the hands of one's enemies. Jesus was "delivered *into* the hands of men" (Matt. 17:22) to be killed, but it is through His triumph over sin and death that God has delivered us *from* darkness *into* the kingdom of His Son. (cf. Col. 1:13) He also delivers us from death (cf. Rom. 7:24) and from the evil of this world. (cf. Gal. 1:4) At the end of time, this deliverance will be manifested once for all when we are delivered "from the wrath to come." (1 Th. 1:10) The mission of the Church is directed to this eternal goal: the salvation of souls from the dominion of sin and death.

When we pray to be delivered from evil, it is not just abstract evil we are speaking of; we also mean the Evil One, Satan. (cf. John 17:15) In this petition, the Church prays to God to show forth the victory over Satan which has already been won. This victory is shown in our own lives when we become "conquerors" (Rom. 8:37) with Christ over Satan and sin. (cf. Rev. 2-3; 12:10-12; 15:2; 21:6-7) This victory is experienced in daily deliverance from Satan and in that definitive freedom to be enjoyed in Heaven. (cf. *Catechism* 2864)

"For the kingdom..."

After the Our Father, the priest says aloud a prayer (called an *embolism*, from the Greek for "an insertion") which is connected to that last petition, to be delivered from evil. At the end of this prayer, we say a concluding doxology:

Quia tuum est regnum, et potéstas, et glória in sǽcula.

For the kingdom, the power	*1 Chr. 29:11; Rev. 1:6; 4:11; 5:12-13*
and the glory are yours now and forever.	*Rev. 7:12; 12:10; 19:1*

This response is a return to the first three petitions of the Our Father: the kingdom (thy kingdom come), the power (thy will be done), and the glory (hallowed by thy name). We do not end the Our Father by simply saying "Amen," but by reaffirming God's primacy in our prayers and in our lives.

These words do not come from Scripture as part of the Lord's Prayer, although some versions of the Bible include them in Matthew 6:13. It appears that this phrase is not present in the older copies of Matthew's gospel, but rather originated in various liturgies and was added by a scribe as a gloss (a comment or note in the margin) in some later copies of Matthew:

> Very early on, liturgical usage concluded the Lord's Prayer with a doxology. In the *Didache*, we find, "For yours are the power and the glory for ever." (*Didache* VIII, 2) The *Apostolic Constitutions* add to the beginning: "the kingdom," and this is the formula retained to our day in ecumenical prayer. (*Apostolic Constitutions*, VII, 24, 1) The Byzantine tradition adds after "the glory" the words "Father, Son, and Holy Spirit." (*Catechism* 2760)

St. Cyril of Jerusalem, who wrote a series of catechetical lectures around A.D. 350, does not mention this closing doxology in his lecture on the Our Father. In the Tradition of the Church, these words are not from the mouth of Christ himself. It is possible they were inspired by the prayer of King David:

> Therefore David blessed the LORD in the presence of all the assembly; and David said: "Blessed are you, O LORD, the God of Israel our father, for ever and ever. Yours, O LORD, is the greatness, and *the power*, and *the glory*, and the victory, and the majesty; for all that is in the heavens and in the earth is yours; yours is *the kingdom*, O LORD, and you are exalted as head above all. Both riches and honor come from you, and you rule over all. In your hand are power and might; and in your hand it is to make great and to give strength to all. And now we thank you, our God, and praise your glorious name." (1 Chr. 29:10-13)

Whatever its origin, its meaning is clear. By praying these words, we deny Satan – "the ruler of this world" (John 12:31) – the kingship, power, and glory that he falsely claims for his own (cf. Luke 4:5-7), and affirm that God is the powerful and glorious King over all creation.

Sign of Peace

The priest says another prayer, in which he invokes the greeting of peace which Jesus gave to His Apostles. The priest then offers us the peace of the Lord, and we reply "And with your spirit." Then he or the deacon may invite us to offer to one another a sign of that peace (but this is optional). While the *Roman Missal* does not define the words to say to one another, these words are suggested:

Pax Dómini sit semper tecum.

The peace of the Lord be with you always.　　　*Gal. 1:3; Phil. 4:7; 2 John 1:3*

to which we should respond "Amen." Common variants of this greeting are "Peace be with you" and "Peace of Christ be with you."

St. Paul wrote eloquently to the Philippians about how God and peace are inseparable:

> Have no anxiety about anything, but in everything by prayer and supplication with thanksgiving let your requests be made known to God. And *the peace of God*, which passes all understanding, will keep your hearts and your minds in Christ Jesus. Finally, brethren, whatever is true, whatever is honorable, whatever is just, whatever is pure, whatever is lovely, whatever is gracious, if there is any excellence, if there is anything worthy of praise, think about these things. What you have learned and received and heard and seen in me, do; and *the God of peace* will be with you. (Phil. 4:6-9)

The peace of God comes to us when we let go of worry and anxiety, and prayerfully place our trust in God. God, Who is the source of peace, comes to us when we focus our minds on the virtuous example of Jesus and the saints and imitate them.

It is important to be reconciled not only to God but to one another before we receive Communion. St. Augustine explained why:

> Christ the Lord ... consecrated the sacrament of our peace and unity upon his table. Who accepts the sacrament of unity, and *keeps not the bond of peace*, does not receive the sacrament for his good, but as *a testimony against himself!*

141

While different Rites of the Church place the Sign of Peace in different places, it is important to recognize the necessity of being at peace when offering sacrifice to the Lord:

> "So if you are offering your gift at the altar, and there remember that your brother has something against you, leave your gift there before the altar and go; *first be reconciled to your brother*, and then come and offer your gift." (Matt. 5:23-24)

The Sign of Peace is not intended to be a "break" in the Liturgy of the Eucharist, a liturgical pause between the Our Father and the Lamb of God. Nor is it supposed to be a social interlude for catching up with old friends. This part of the Mass is a manifestation of the unity and peace we have with Christ and all those Who belong to Him. It is a liturgical action meant to express "peace, communion, and charity" (GIRM 154) to one another. While a hug or kiss may be appropriate between close relations, this is not a time to make people uncomfortable by "invading their personal space." It is appropriate to "offer the sign of peace only to those who are nearest and in a sober manner." (GIRM 82)

"Lamb of God"

After the Sign of Peace, the priest or choir intones the Lamb of God, the *Agnus Dei*:

Agnus Dei, qui tollis peccáta mundi: miserére nobis.
Agnus Dei, qui tollis peccáta mundi: miserére nobis.
Agnus Dei, qui tollis peccáta mundi: dona nobis pacem.

Lamb of God,	*Gen. 22:8; Ex. 12*
you take away the sins of the world, have mercy on us.	*Lev. 16:21*
Lamb of God,	*Rev. 5:6*
you take away the sins of the world, have mercy on us.	*John 1:29*
Lamb of God,	*1 Cor. 5:7; 1 Pet. 1:19*
you take away the sins of the world, grant us peace.	*John 14:27; 20:26*

While this ancient chant is being sung, the priest is performing the Fraction Rite, breaking the primary Host into fragments. This represents the breaking of Christ's body (though not His bones, cf. John 19:32-36) on the cross, and it calls to mind the breaking of the bread which Jesus did at the Last Supper and at Emmaus. The *Agnus Dei* can go on as long as needed to accompany the Fraction, singing the first verse as many times as necessary (at least twice), but the final verse is always "Lamb of God ... grant us peace."

We first called Christ the "Lamb of God" in the *Gloria*. This title is deeply significant and ancient in its origin, reaching back to Abraham, the first of the Patriarchs of Israel. God tested Abraham, asking him to offer his only son Isaac as a sacrifice. Isaac, bearing the wood for the sacrifice on his back as he and Abraham walked up the mountain, asked his father where the lamb to be offered was; Abraham replied "God will provide himself the lamb." (Gen. 22:8) What Abraham found was no lamb, but a ram with its horns caught in a thicket.[3] From that time on, God's people sought the "lamb of God."

To commemorate His liberating the Hebrews from Egypt, God instituted the feast of Passover at which every family was to take a pure, unblemished lamb and kill it, marking their doorposts with its blood and roasting and eating its flesh. (cf. Ex. 12) In time, Jerusalem maintained a sacrificial flock of Temple lambs so that families on pilgrimage for the Passover could be sure to have a pure and unblemished lamb (rather than bringing one with them on the journey). Still, these lambs were not *God's* lamb, but each family's lambs.[4]

It was not until St. John the Baptist cried out, "Behold, the Lamb of God!" (John 1:29, 36) that the fulfillment of this ancient promise was made known. This title, which might sound peculiar and obscure to our modern ears, would have rung loud and clear in the ears of the Jews to whom St. John spoke. And he was not the only one to make such a clear connection between Christ and the Passover lamb. St. Paul, writing to the Corinthians, announced that "Christ, *our paschal lamb*, has been sacrificed." (1 Cor. 5:7)[5] St. Peter wrote that we have been ransomed "with the precious blood of Christ, like that of *a lamb without blemish or spot*." (1 Pet. 1:19) And St. John the Apostle and Evangelist, in his book of Revelation, refers to Jesus as "the Lamb" nearly thirty times, most

---

[3] This scene is rich in Christological symbolism: Christ, like Isaac, bore the wood for His own sacrifice on His back, and He wore a crown of thorns, prefigured by the ram whose horns were caught in a thorn-bush.

[4] The ritual of the Passover also points to Christ: He, like the lamb, is pure and without blemish, and His bones were not broken when He was sacrificed.

[5] "Paschal" (as in "Paschal mystery") comes from the Greek word *pascha*, which comes from the Hebrew word *pesach*, which means "Passover."

notably describing His appearance as "a Lamb standing, as though it had been slain." (Rev. 5:6)

It is this Lamb of God, Jesus Christ, Who "takes away the sin of the world" by His self-sacrifice. (John 1:29) Every time we say that Jesus "take[s] away the sins of the world," we should be aware that we are speaking in the *present* tense, not the *past* tense. This is a reminder that Christ's work of redemption did not conclude with His death, but is continual and ongoing: the Mass is offered for the expiation of our sins.

We should remember that, after the consecration, Jesus Christ is present sacramentally on the altar in the Eucharist. This prayer, then, is addressed directly to the Blessed Sacrament visible before our very eyes. Recalling the death He endured for our sins, we humbly beg Him to show us His abundant mercy and to give us the peace which the world cannot give. (cf. John 14:27) By addressing Christ in the Eucharist this way, we remind ourselves of the price He paid that we might be able to receive Him in Communion; we are also reminded that Jesus takes away the sins of the *world*, not just *our* sins. (cf. 1 John 2:2)

The priest quietly says a prayer after the Fraction as he places a small piece of the Host into the Chalice. Just as the separate consecration of the bread and wine was a sign of the separation of Christ's body and blood – His true bodily death – this mingling of the Host and the Chalice is a sign of the reunion of His body and blood (or His body and soul) at His Resurrection.

"Lord, I am not worthy..."

After making his private preparation for Holy Communion, the priest holds up the Host (and possibly the Chalice as well) and shows it to us for our adoration. He announces the Lamb of God (cf. John 1:29) and the marriage supper of the Lamb. (cf. Rev. 19:6-9) We reply with words from Scripture as well:

Dómine, non sum dignus, ut intres sub téctum meum, sed tantum dic verbo, et sanábitur ánima mea.

» Lord, I am not worthy that you should enter under my roof,   *Matt. 8:8*
» but only say the word and my soul shall be healed.

This prayer is *our* liturgical preparation for receiving Communion. There are two changes to the translation we are used to; both deserve our close attention.

Enter Under My Roof

The old translation said "worthy to receive you," but the new translation is more faithful to the Latin and to Scripture. The new translation is *not* referring to the roof of our mouths. To meaningfully pray this response, we must be familiar with its context:

> As [Jesus] entered Capernaum, a centurion came forward to him, begging him and saying, "Lord, my servant is lying paralyzed at home, in terrible distress." And he said to him, "I will come and heal him." But the centurion answered him, "*Lord, I am not worthy to have you come under my roof; but only say the word, and my servant will be healed.* For I am a man under authority, with soldiers under me; and I say to one, 'Go,' and he goes, and to another, 'Come,' and he comes, and to my slave, 'Do this,' and he does it." When Jesus heard him, he marveled, and said to those who followed him, "Truly, I say to you, not even in Israel have I found such faith." … And to the centurion Jesus said, "Go; let it be done for you as you have believed." And the servant was healed at that very moment. (Matt. 8:5-10, 13)

The statement of the centurion was an expression of his great faith in the power that Jesus had. The centurion believed that Jesus did not need to travel and enter his house, but had the ability to cure his servant by simply willing it and saying it. To come under the roof means to enter the house, implying a familiar relationship. But even more important is that according to Jewish ritual law, entering the house of a Gentile would have made Jesus "impure." (cf. Acts 10:28)

There is a great spiritual message here. God could have remedied our sorry, fallen state just by willing it, just by *saying* a word. But instead, He *sent* His Word to us, coming under our roof – taking on a body of flesh and our human condition – and suffering ridicule, persecution, and death on a cross. "For our sake he made him to be sin who knew no sin, so that in him we might become the righteousness of God." (2 Cor. 5:21)

So what roof do *we* mean? We are temples of the Holy Spirit, and our flesh is like the "roof" of this temple. We know we are unworthy to be such temples, where God is present *spiritually*; we are even less worthy to receive our Lord in the Blessed Sacrament. But here Christ does for us what He did not do for the centurion, not because our faith is any less (although oftentimes it is), but because "God had foreseen something better for us." (Heb. 11:40) Jesus gladly comes to us in the Eucharist.

My Soul Shall be Healed

We also say "*my soul* shall be healed," instead of just "*I* shall be healed." This does not mean we are distinguishing the soul from the rest of our person, for the Latin word *anima* means more than just "soul." It also means "mind" and "vital principle." Our soul is, in a way, our identity. Being healed in our soul is more radical than simply being healed bodily (which is great, but could be superficial); it is being healed at our core. A healed soul manifests its wholeness throughout the rest of our being.

There are many fruits of receiving Holy Communion devoutly: it increases our union with Christ, it strengthens our spiritual life (in the way material food strengthens our bodily life), it separates us from sin, it wipes away *venial* sin (but not *mortal* sin,[6] which is forgiven through the sacrament of Reconciliation), and it strengthens us against committing future mortal sin. (cf. *Catechism* 1391-1395) This is the healing our souls experience when we receive the Precious Body and Blood of our Lord.

Posture

The standard posture in the United States (unless the Bishop decides otherwise) is to kneel after the *Agnus Dei*. Kneeling as we are shown the Blessed Sacrament, to adore it and profess our unworthiness to receive it, is a sign of our contrition and dependence on God, Who alone makes us clean and heals the blemishes on our souls.

The Extraordinary Form of the Mass includes a three-fold striking of the breast while this response is said three times. Although it is not presently prescribed in the Ordinary Form of the Mass, Pope Benedict, writing before his election to the papacy, considered that at this moment, "we look upon him who is the Shepherd and for us became the Lamb and, as Lamb, bore our iniquities" and that "it is only right and proper that we should strike our breasts and remind ourselves, even physically, that our iniquities lay on his shoulders, that 'with his stripes we are

---

[6] "Mortal sin is sin whose object is grave matter and which is also committed with full knowledge and deliberate consent." (*Catechism* 1857) For more on the difference between venial and mortal sin, see *Catechism* 1854-1864, especially 1858-1861.

healed.'" (*The Spirit of the Liturgy*, p. 207) Rev. Romano Guardini also wrote of this gesture that, when done before Communion, "it is a summons to repentance and to the self-inflicted punishment of a contrite heart." (*Sacred Signs*) This gesture may be done as a personal devotion, but it is possible that in the future this pious tradition will be universally re-incorporated into the Roman liturgy.

Holy Communion

A peculiar coincidence in Latin is that the verbs for "to be" and "to eat" are both spelled *esse*. These verbs are irregular, and they are not always conjugated the same way; for instance, "I am" is *sum*, whereas "I eat" is *edo*. However, "you are" and "you eat" are rendered the same way: *es* (for singular you) or *estis* (for plural you). That means the well-known expression "you are what you eat" can be said in Latin as "*quod es, es*" or "*quod estis, estis.*" This phrase takes on a whole new meaning when you consider what it is you are eating when you receive Holy Communion.

When we come up to receive our Lord, we should do so reverently. We stand or kneel before the minister of Holy Communion; if we receive standing, we are to make a sign of reverence first (a bow of the head). Then the minister says "The Body of Christ" or "The Blood of Christ" (depending on what form we are receiving) and we respond "Amen."

For St. Augustine, these words are our mystery:

> If, therefore, you are the body of Christ and its members, *your* mystery is placed on the Lord's table: you receive *your* mystery. To that which you are [or: *to that which you eat*], you answer "Amen," and, thus answering, you assent. That is, you hear "The body of Christ," and you answer "Amen." Therefore, *be* a member of the body of Christ, that the "Amen" may be true!

St. Augustine was not belittling the awesome presence of Jesus Christ in the Eucharist, but he was reminding his congregation that the Body of Christ is both *His* flesh and blood and *our* identity. We, who belong to the Church which is the mystical Body of Christ, are receiving food which is unlike any other food. When we eat natural food, it becomes part of us; when we eat this spiritual food, *we* become part of *it*.

He explains that this change, this identifying of ourselves with this heavenly Bread, is foreshadowed in our initiation into the Church:

> When you were being exorcised, it is as though you were being ground up. When you were baptized, it is as though you were mixed together [into dough]. When you received the fire of the Holy Spirit, it is as though you were being baked. *Be* that which you *see*, and *receive* that which you *are!* *That* is what the Apostle spoke concerning the bread.

St. Paul said that just as there is one bread made from many grains, we, though many, are one body. This "bread" and this "body" are one and the same. What we see, though it looks like bread, is the Body of Christ, and we were called out of darkness to be a member of that Body; therefore, in receiving the Body of Christ in Holy Communion, we are receiving *Who* we are!

But there is a warning attached to the invitation. The priest says "Blessed are *those* who are called to the supper of the Lamb." We are not all indiscriminately called to receive Holy Communion. Some of us are not properly disposed to receive it; we are called, instead, to Penance and the sacrament of Confession. St. Paul knew this and taught it explicitly to the Church in Corinth:

> Whoever, therefore, eats the bread or drinks the cup of the Lord in an unworthy manner will be guilty of profaning the body and blood of the Lord. Let a man examine himself, and so eat of the bread and drink of the cup. For any one who eats and drinks without discerning the body *eats and drinks judgment* upon himself. (1 Cor. 11:27-29)

This warning is relayed by St. Augustine:

> Who accepts the sacrament of unity, and keeps not the bond of peace, does not receive the sacrament for his good, but as *a testimony against himself!*

If we are not at peace with the Body of Christ (because of grave sin), we are not receiving a sacrament of unity but a testament to our separation from that Body: in receiving what we have prevented ourselves from being (*one* body) we are, as St. Paul describes it, "guilty of profaning the body and blood of the Lord."

The word "profane" literally means "outside" (*pro-*) "the temple" (*fanum*). It is the opposite of the word "sacred." We are *supposed* to be temples of the Holy Spirit, a proper dwelling place for the Body of Christ. All sin is opposed to holiness, but mortal sin is what cuts that communion off between us and God. When we are guilty of mortal sin, we are sorely in need of Jesus to come and "cleanse the temple" of that which is profaning it, lest *we* profane the *Eucharist* by accepting it unworthily.

Spiritual Communion

The custom, in some places, of going up to receive a blessing instead of Communion during the Communion procession is not an official part of the rite. It is currently under the study of the Congregation for Divine Worship and the Discipline of the Sacraments, and should generally be avoided. If you are not receiving Communion (for whatever reason), the long-standing tradition in the Church is to stay where you are and make a prayer of "spiritual communion." Here is one such prayer:

> My Jesus,
> I believe that You are present in the Most Holy Sacrament.
> I love You above all things,
> and I desire to receive You into my soul.
>
> Since I cannot at this moment receive You sacramentally,
> come at least spiritually into my heart.
>
> I embrace You as if You were already there
> and unite myself wholly to You.
> Never permit me to be separated from You.
> Amen.

During the Communion procession, a hymn or chant may be sung. Our posture when we have returned to our pews is up to us, but many choose to remain kneeling in prayer at least until the Blessed Sacrament has been placed back in the tabernacle and the door to the tabernacle is closed. There should be ample time for private, silent prayer of thanksgiving after Communion, but there may also be a hymn of thanksgiving (preferably sung by the whole congregation) at this time.

Then we rise for the Post-Communion prayer. The Collect prayer collects our private intentions and prayers and joins them to the intention of this particular celebration of the Mass, and the Prayer over the Offerings presents the bread and wine to God in the context of that same celebration. The Post-Communion Prayer thanks God for the gift of the sacrament we have received, usually by calling attention to the heavenly reality anticipated by it. It also summarizes the mysteries that were celebrated and prepares us for what we will be undertaking when we go out into the world. We respond "Amen," and then the Mass nears its end, but what happens at the end of the liturgy is just the beginning of something else.

Questions for Reflection

1) **Interpret:** Why is the revelation of God as Father, as "Daddy," a turning point in salvation history? What do we learn about God and about ourselves by this?

2) **Interpret:** Lambs were commonly used by Israel for sacrifices. What images might a 1st-century Jew have thought of when he heard St. John the Baptist point to Jesus and say, "Behold the Lamb of God who takes away the sin of the world" (John 1:29)? What images come to *your* mind when you hear "Lamb of God"?

3) **Interpret:** When Christ appeared after the Resurrection, He told His Apostles, "Peace be with you." (John 20:19) Almost every epistle in the New Testament begins with a greeting involving peace from God through Jesus Christ. What is the relationship of peace (with God and one another) to salvation? What kind of peace is this?

4) **Explain:** There are many spiritual interpretations of the Fraction Rite and the joining of the two species (bread and wine) in the Chalice. What significance do you see in these two acts?

5) **Explain:** The sign of peace described in the New Testament epistles is called a "holy kiss" (Rom. 16:16) in contrast to the kiss of betrayal delivered by Judas. (cf. Luke 22:47-48) How is a kiss, or a handshake, or a stylized embrace (as is the custom in Rome) a *real* sign of Christian peace, instead of an empty social gesture?

6) **Explain:** How is Holy Communion the "marriage supper of the Lamb"? (Rev. 19:9) To whom is the Lamb married?

7) **Relate:** When else do you pray the Our Father? Has this prayer taken on new meaning as you've grown in your faith?

8) **Relate:** Why is it customary in some places for children who are receiving their first Holy Communion to be dressed as though for

a wedding? What should our demeanor and appearance at Mass convey, especially as we receive Communion?

9) **Relate:** How is the Eucharist a *private* encounter with Christ? How is it a *communal* encounter with Christ? How can you share your encounter with those who are not Catholic?

I heard the voice of the Lord saying,
"Whom shall I send, and who will go for us?"
Then I said, "Here am I! Send me."
(Isaiah 6:8)

"Go therefore and make disciples of all nations, baptizing them
in the name of the Father and of the Son and of the Holy Spirit,
teaching them to observe all that I have commanded you."
(Matthew 28:19-20)

12

Concluding Rite

REMEMBER HOW THE beginning of Mass is like the entrance of Jesus into Jerusalem, and the Penitential Act is like the cleansing of the Temple? The end of Mass brings us through the forty days of Christ's time on earth after His Resurrection. We are there on the mountain in Galilee where Jesus gave His Apostles the great commission (cf. Matt. 28:18-20), and we are there on the Mount of Olives where He blessed them and ascended into Heaven. The priest gives us a Trinitarian blessing and dismisses us... but when do we receive a mission as the Apostles did?

The answer to that question is found in the name which the Roman Rite gives to the Divine Liturgy: the *Mass.* It comes from the Latin word *missa*, which is one of the words the priest says at the end of Mass: "*Ite, missa est*," which literally means, "Go, it is the dismissal." Why would we name this liturgy after what is practically the last word said, the last part of the Mass? Pope Benedict XVI, in *Sacramentum Caritatis*, explains the significance of this word *missa*:

> After the blessing, the deacon or the priest dismisses the people with the words: *Ite, missa est.* These words help us to grasp the relationship between the Mass just celebrated and the mission of

Christians in the world. In antiquity, *missa* simply meant "dismissal." However in Christian usage it gradually took on a deeper meaning. The word "dismissal" has come to imply a "mission." *These few words succinctly express the missionary nature of the Church.* The People of God might be helped to understand more clearly this essential dimension of the Church's life, taking the dismissal as a starting-point. (SC 51)

The word "dismissal" is related to "mission" which comes from the Latin word *missa* which gives us the word "Mass"! The dismissal is not just a sending-forth, it is a sending-forth on a mission, the mission of the Church, delivered to the Apostles by Jesus before He ascended into Heaven: "Go therefore and *make disciples* of all nations, *baptizing them* in the name of the Father and of the Son and of the Holy Spirit, *teaching them* to observe all that I have commanded you." (Matt. 28:19-20)

The end of Mass is the renewal of that mission by the members of the Church, and it is *quite* a mission to undertake. How can we hope to be successful in it? While the primary purpose of Mass is to worship God, He graciously bestows graces to us through it, and it is these graces we receive during Mass which make this mission of ours possible. First, let's look at the parts of the Concluding Rite.

Dialogue

The priest or bishop says "The Lord be with you," and we reply, "And with your spirit." If a bishop is celebrating Mass, there is an additional dialogue between him and the congregation. This dialogue, like Form B of the Penitential Act, is a call-and-response based on the Psalms. He will first say "Blessed be the name of the Lord," to which we respond:

Ex hoc nunc et usque in sǽculum.

Now and forever. *Ps. 113:2*

Then the bishop says "Our help is in the name of the Lord," to which we respond:

Qui fecit cǽlum et terram.

Who made heaven and earth. *Ps. 124:8*

Both of these verses have to do with the *name* of the Lord. His name is blessed forever, and not only by angels, but by us mere humans as well.

Remember that in the Our Father, the first petition we pray is that His name be hallowed; at a pontifical Mass (one celebrated by a bishop), we already begin fulfilling that petition with these words of praise at the end of Mass.

It is in the name of the almighty Creator of everything that was, is, and will be, that we find our help. If God can create the heavens and the earth out of nothing, surely this same God can help us in our daily lives to overcome temptations, struggles, and every sin which drags us down and pulls us away from Him. When we pray these words with a bishop, we are calling upon God as one people, His people, blessing His name and asking for His help.

Final Blessing

The priest or bishop then bestows the final blessing on us. There may be a series of invocations to which we respond "Amen," but the blessing always ends with the Sign of the Cross.

Here we are receiving that great blessing which Christ bestowed on His disciples as He ascended into Heaven. (cf. Luke 24:50-51) A priestly blessing has great power because it is given to us by a man acting in the person of Christ by virtue of his ordination. As we make the Sign of the Cross over our bodies, we should consider once more just *what* sign it is that we place on ourselves as a "blessing."

A Blessing in Disguise

How is the Cross a blessing? Isn't the Cross a burden, a curse, and a punishment?

The cross is where the Church finds her mission. Jesus gave up His body and shed his blood for the remission of the sins of the whole world. He made this great sacrifice on the Cross, and we are being sent out into the world to preach His Gospel, including the proclamation of His death: "We preach Christ crucified." (1 Cor. 1:23) "For I decided to know nothing among you except Jesus Christ and him crucified." (1 Cor. 2:2) It is by the Cross of Christ that we have been made heirs of the blessing promised to Abraham. (cf. Gal. 3:13-14)

At the beginning of Mass, we make the Sign of the Cross as a way of showing our solidarity with the suffering of Christ, into Whose death we were baptized, taking up our crosses and following Him. At the end of Mass, we reaffirm that solidarity and once more take up our crosses, with renewed strength and grace because of our devout participation in the Sacrifice of the Mass.

Dismissal

The bishop, priest, or deacon then gives us the dismissal. There are four texts that can be used – the traditional words being "*Ite, missa est*," which means "Go, it is the dismissal" – but whatever they say, our response is:

Deo grátias.

Thanks be to God.   *Luke 24:53; Rom. 6:7; 2 Cor. 2:14; 1 Th. 2:13*

During the Octave of Easter and on Pentecost, the words of dismissal and our response is followed by "Alleluia, Alleluia!"

Now, as was the case with our response to the readings of Scripture ("Thanks be to God"), we need to know *why* we're thanking God. Too often – perhaps because of a long homily, or music we didn't like, or a crying child, or a television program we don't want to miss – we're saying "Thank God I can go *home* now!" But as was made clear at the beginning of this chapter, that's *not* what the dismissal is about. Remember that the dismissal of the Mass is a celebration of Christ's ascending to His Father and of our receiving the great commission.

Although the Mass is a powerful tool of evangelization, it's not the only way to evangelize. Indeed, someone might get utterly confused if he comes to Mass without knowing the "backstory," even to the point of not coming back again, and that's not what God wants! Part of our mission is to prepare others for what and *Whom* they will encounter in the Mass. That's why there are so many lay apostolates and religious orders concerned with preaching and apologetics and catechesis. We need to bring with us from the Mass that "which we have heard, which we have seen with our eyes, which we have looked upon and touched with our hands, concerning the word of life" (1 John 1:1) and share that with everyone we meet. But before we go out into the world, we should take a moment to consider what the disciples did before they went out on their mission.

What did the disciples do after Jesus ascended into Heaven? They "returned to Jerusalem with *great joy,* and were continually *in the temple blessing God.*" (Luke 24:52-53) This is why we say "Thanks be to God" at the end of the Mass. We're not glad the Mass is over, we're glad that we have received the graces necessary to go out into the world and bring souls to Christ. We thank Him for calling us into His family, to have a share in the "family business," working in His vineyard, being fishers of men. We thank Him for making us co-workers in the mission He has had in mind since the beginning of time.

And perhaps we should follow the example of the disciples more closely. After your next Mass, after the recessional hymn has ended, imitate the disciples and stay "in the temple blessing God." Remain for just a few moments, either at your seat or in front of the tabernacle, and praise God. It might be hard — there might be distractions from other people — but give a few more moments to God. Who knows, perhaps others will see your light shining, and they too will join you in glorifying their Father in Heaven.

At the beginning of this final chapter, I mentioned the graces we receive during the Mass as being the driving force behind our ability to carry out the mission of the Church successfully. Elsewhere in this book, I have written of the Mass as a sort of grand exchange between God and man, between Heaven and earth. What are these graces? What exactly is being exchanged between us and Him?

God draws us to Him and we respond by coming to worship Him. We bring our sinfulness to Him and He gives us **His mercy**. We praise Him and collect our prayers together and present them to Him and He begins to answer with **His Word**. During the Liturgy of the Eucharist, we offer Him bread and wine which He accepts, and by the power of His Holy Spirit, they become the Eucharist. The priest offers the Eucharist to God and He returns it to us; with Christ present on the altar, we place before God our troubles, our worries, and our anxieties, and He gives us **His peace**. Celebrating that peace, we worship the Lamb of God Who takes away the sins of the world, and God, Who once gave His Son over to us to be crucified, now gives Him to us again as the Bread of Life, our spiritual food: God gives us **His very Self**, His Body, Blood, Soul, and Divinity, His Real Presence in the Eucharist. We are walking, living tabernacles of the Lord after receiving Communion! We respond with our own private Eucharistic prayers (prayers of thanks). Finally, God gives us **His blessing**, and with that we say "Thank you!" one more time before going forth in joy to show the love of Christ which He wants to extend to every single person.

These are the five great graces we receive from God in the Mass: His mercy, His Word, His peace, His Self, and His blessing. These five graces are what sustain us for carrying out the mission of evangelization which the Church has promised to fulfill in every age, throughout the whole world. These five graces are part of the Gospel message that we are called to preach, which is why God brings us into contact with them at every Mass.

Such a mission requires that we prepare ourselves with prayer… and what better way is there to prepare than by *praying* the Mass?

Questions for Reflection

1) **Interpret:** Christ has not left His Church alone. What did He promise to send to us after His Ascension? How does this gift help the Church bring salvation to the world?

2) **Explain:** Rev. Romano Guardini wrote that standing is "the sign of vigilance and *action*" showing the respect "of the *soldier* on duty." Why do we stand for the dismissal?

3) **Explain:** How does the liturgy use signs and symbols that are familiar to our everyday life? What new meanings does it give them? Which signs and symbols are unfamiliar to us? Why does the Church use unfamiliar symbols?

4) **Relate:** The Mass is not primarily a teaching tool, but it *does* teach us how the Church prays and what she believes. What have you learned about the faith by learning more about the Mass?

5) **Relate:** How do you see the Mass differently now? What can you share with your family and friends?

APPENDIX
How We Offer the Eucharist

O N NOVEMBER 20, 1947, Pope Pius XII (the predecessor to Bl. Pope John XXIII) promulgated an encyclical on the liturgy, *Mediator Dei*. Over 200 paragraphs in length, this encyclical was an artful treatment of the liturgy as the act of the whole Church. It is an important backdrop for understanding the liturgical renewal called for by Vatican II.

Mediator Dei of Pope Pius XII

The lengthy excerpt below is from paragraphs 80-104 of *Mediator Dei*. In them, Pope Pius XII describes the manner in which the laity participate in the offering of the Eucharist to the Father. By cultivating the liturgical spirituality he describes, you will come to see the Eucharistic Prayer as something involving not just your attention, but your *intention* as well.

> All the faithful should be aware that to participate in the Eucharistic sacrifice is their chief duty and supreme dignity, and that not in an inert and negligent fashion, giving way to distractions and day-dreaming, but with such earnestness and concentration that they may be united as closely as possible with the High Priest, according to the Apostle, "have this mind among yourselves, which was in Christ Jesus." (Phil. 2:5) And together with Him and through Him let them make their oblation, and in union with Him let them offer up themselves.

It is quite true that Christ is a priest; but He is a priest not for Himself but for us, when in the name of the whole human race He offers our prayers and religious homage to the eternal Father; He is also a victim and for us since He substitutes Himself for sinful man. Now the exhortation of the Apostle, "Let this mind be in you which was also in Christ Jesus," requires that all Christians should possess, as far as is humanly possible, the same dispositions as those which the divine Redeemer had when He offered Himself in sacrifice: that is to say, they should in a humble attitude of mind, pay adoration, honor, praise and thanksgiving to the supreme majesty of God. Moreover, it means that they must assume to some extent the character of a victim, that they deny themselves as the Gospel commands, that freely and of their own accord they do penance and that each detests and satisfies for his sins. It means, in a word, that we must all undergo with Christ a mystical death on the cross so that we can apply to ourselves the words of St. Paul, "With Christ I am nailed to the cross." (Gal. 2:19)

The fact, however, that the faithful participate in the Eucharistic sacrifice does not mean that they also are endowed with priestly power. ... The priest acts for the people only because he represents Jesus Christ, who is Head of all His members and offers Himself in their stead. Hence, he goes to the altar as the minister of Christ, inferior to Christ but superior to the people.[1]
...

However, it must also be said that the faithful do offer the divine Victim, though in a different sense. ... The rites and prayers of the Eucharistic sacrifice signify and show no less clearly that the oblation of the Victim is made by the priests in company with the people. For not only does the sacred minister, after the oblation of the bread and wine when he turns to the people, say the significant prayer: "Pray brethren, that my sacrifice and yours may be acceptable to God the Father Almighty;" but also the prayers by which the divine Victim is offered to God are generally expressed in the plural number: and in these it is indicated more than once that the people also participate in this august sacrifice inasmuch as they offer the same. ...

It is fitting, then, that the Christian people should also desire to know in what sense they are said in the canon of the Mass to offer

---

[1] "*Christo inferiorem, superiorem autem populo.*" The Latin words *inferiorem* and *superiorem* do not mean the same as "inferior" and "superior" in terms of excellence (as if a priest is a "better" person than a layman) but rather denote "under" and "over" in terms of hierarchical ordering. In the Church, certain people are "over" others, as St. Paul explained to the Thessalonians: "respect those who labor among you and *are over you in the Lord* and admonish you." (1 Th. 5:12)

up the sacrifice. ... In this most important subject it is necessary, in order to avoid giving rise to a dangerous error, that we define the exact meaning of the word "offer."

The unbloody immolation at the words of consecration, when Christ is made present upon the altar in the state of a victim, is performed by the priest and by him alone, as the representative of Christ and not as the representative of the faithful. But it is because the priest places the divine victim upon the altar that he offers it to God the Father as an oblation for the glory of the Blessed Trinity and for the good of the whole Church. Now the faithful participate in the oblation, understood in this limited sense, after their own fashion and in a twofold manner, namely, because they not only offer the sacrifice by the hands of the priest, but also, to a certain extent, in union with him. It is by reason of this participation that the offering made by the people is also included in liturgical worship.

Now it is clear that the faithful offer the sacrifice by the hands of the priest from the fact that the minister at the altar, in offering a sacrifice in the name of all His members, represents Christ, the Head of the Mystical Body. Hence the whole Church can rightly be said to offer up the victim through Christ. But the conclusion that the people offer the sacrifice with the priest himself is not based on the fact that, being members of the Church no less than the priest himself, they perform a visible liturgical rite; for this is the privilege only of the minister who has been divinely appointed to this office: rather it is based on the fact that the people unite their hearts in praise, impetration, expiation and thanksgiving[2] with the prayers or intention of the priest, even of the High Priest himself, so that in the one and same offering of the victim and according to a visible sacerdotal rite, they may be presented to God the Father. It is obviously necessary that the external sacrificial rite should, of its very nature, signify the internal worship of the heart. Now the sacrifice of the New Law signifies that supreme worship by which the principal Offerer himself, who is Christ, and, in union with Him and through Him, all the members of the Mystical Body pay God the honor and reverence that are due to Him. ...

In order that the oblation by which the faithful offer the divine Victim in this sacrifice to the heavenly Father may have its full effect, it is necessary that the people add something else, namely, the offering of themselves as a victim. This offering in fact is not confined merely to the liturgical sacrifice. For the Prince of the Apostles wishes us, as living stones built upon Christ, the

---

[2] These are the four ends of the Mass (glory, petition, expiation, and thanksgiving).

cornerstone, to be able as "a holy priesthood, to offer up spiritual sacrifices, acceptable to God by Jesus Christ." (1 Pet. 2:5) ... At that time especially when the faithful take part in the liturgical service with such piety and recollection that it can truly be said of them: "whose faith and devotion is known to Thee," (Roman Canon) it is then, with the High Priest and through Him they offer themselves as a spiritual sacrifice, that each one's faith ought to become more ready to work through charity, his piety more real and fervent, and each one should consecrate himself to the furthering of the divine glory, desiring to become as like as possible to Christ in His most grievous sufferings. ...

Let the faithful, therefore, consider to what a high dignity they are raised by the sacrament of Baptism. They should not think it enough to participate in the Eucharistic sacrifice with that general intention which befits members of Christ and children of the Church, but let them further, in keeping with the spirit of the sacred liturgy, be most closely united with the High Priest and His earthly minister, at the time the consecration of the divine Victim is enacted, and at that time especially when those solemn words are pronounced, "By Him and with Him and in Him is to Thee, God the Father almighty, in the unity of the Holy Ghost, all honor and glory for ever and ever"; to these words in fact the people answer, "Amen." Nor should Christians forget to offer themselves, their cares, their sorrows, their distress and their necessities in union with their divine Savior upon the cross.

Second Vatican Council

This theme of the laity offering the Eucharist to God through and with the priest, and joining themselves to that offering, is echoed in multiple documents of the Second Vatican Council.

Constitution on the Sacred Liturgy

[B]y offering the Immaculate Victim, not only through the hands of the priest, but also with him, they should learn also *to offer themselves*. (*Sacrosanctum Concilium* 48)

Dogmatic Constitution on the Church

Taking part in the Eucharistic sacrifice, which is the fount and apex of the whole Christian life, they offer the Divine Victim to God, and *offer themselves along with It*. (*Lumen Gentium* 11)

For all their works, prayers and apostolic endeavors, their ordinary married and family life, their daily occupations, their physical and mental relaxation, if carried out in the Spirit, and even the hardships of life, if patiently borne – all these become "spiritual sacrifices acceptable to God through Jesus Christ." Together with the offering of the Lord's body, *they are most fittingly offered* in the celebration of the Eucharist. (*Lumen Gentium* 34)

Decree on the Ministry and Life of Priests

Through the ministry of the priests, the *spiritual sacrifice of the faithful* is made *perfect in union with the sacrifice of Christ* [Who] is offered sacramentally in the Eucharist... (*Presbyterorum Ordinis* 2)

[P]riests must instruct their people to offer to God the Father the Divine Victim in the Sacrifice of the Mass, and *to join to it the offering of their own lives.* (*Presbyterorum Ordinis* 5)

Dominicae Cenae of Pope John Paul II

In 1980, Pope John Paul II wrote a letter for Holy Thursday on the topic of the Eucharist, titled *Dominicae Cenae.* It included a section explaining the manner in which the faithful join their offerings to that of the priest. It echoes some of the sentiments of Pope Pius XII:

Although all those who participate in the Eucharist do not confect the sacrifice as He does, *they offer with Him*, by virtue of the common priesthood, *their own spiritual sacrifices represented by the bread and wine* from the moment of their presentation at the altar. ...

This sacrificial value is expressed earlier in every celebration by the words with which the priest concludes the presentation of the gifts, asking the faithful to pray "that my sacrifice and yours may be acceptable to God, the almighty Father." ...

All who participate with faith in the Eucharist become aware that it is a "sacrifice," that is to say, a "consecrated Offering." For the bread and wine presented at the altar and *accompanied by the devotion and the spiritual sacrifices of the participants* are finally consecrated, so as to become truly, really and substantially Christ's own body that is given up and His blood that is shed. ...

To this sacrifice, which is renewed in a sacramental form on the altar, the offerings of bread and wine, *united with the devotion of the faithful*, nevertheless bring their unique contribution, since by means of the consecration by the priest they become sacred species. ... "The Church's intention is that the faithful not only offer the spotless victim but also *learn to offer themselves* and daily to be drawn into ever more perfect union, through Christ the Mediator, with the Father and with each other, so that at last God may be all in all." (cf. GIRM 79f.)

It is therefore very opportune and necessary to continue to actuate a new and intense education, in order to discover all the richness contained in the new liturgy. (*Dominicae Cenae* 9)

Bibliography

Benedict XVI, Pope. *Compendium of the Catechism of the Catholic Church.* USCCB Publishing, 2005.

Challoner, Richard, et. al. *The Glories of the Catholic Church, Volume II.* John Duffy, 1895.

Dubruiel, Michael. *The How-To Book of the Mass.* Our Sunday Visitor, 2007.

Elliott, Msgr. Peter J. *Ceremonies of the Modern Roman Rite.* Revised Edition. Ignatius Press, 2005.

Guardini, Rev. Romano. *Sacred Signs.* Pio Decimo Press, 1956.

Hahn, Scott. *The Lamb's Supper.* Doubleday, 1999.

Hahn, Scott and Regis J. Flaherty, eds. *Catholic for a Reason III.* Emmaus Road Publishing, 2004.

John Paul II, Pope. *Catechism of the Catholic Church.* USCCB Publishing, 1997.

Kocik, Rev. Thomas A. *Loving and Living the Mass.* Zaccheus Press, 2007.

Lukefahr, CM, Rev. Oscar. *We Worship: A Guide to the Catholic Mass.* Liguori Publications, 2004.

Oury, Rev. Guy. *The Mass.* Catholic Book Publishing Co., 1988.

Ratzinger, Joseph Cardinal and John Saward, trans. *The Spirit of the Liturgy.* Ignatius Press, 2000.

Sheen, Most Rev. Fulton. J. *Calvary and the Mass.* P.J. Kenedy & Sons, 1936.

Stravinskas, Rev. Peter M. J. *The Bible and the Mass.* Newman House Press, 2001.

Tuberville, DD, Henry. *The Douay Catechism.* Excelsior Catholic Publishing House, 1649.

United States Conference of Catholic Bishops. *General Instruction of the Roman Missal.* USCCB Publishing, 2002.

6202740R0

Made in the USA
Charleston, SC
26 September 2010